Sunrise 47

MICHAEL D. MITCHELL

Outkirts Press, Inc.
Denver, Colorado

The opinions expressed in this manuscript are solely the opinions of the author and do not represent the opinions or thoughts of the publisher. The author has represented and warranted full ownership and/or legal right to publish all the materials in this book.

Sunrise 47
All Rights Reserved.
Copyright © 2009 Michael D. Mitchell
V1.0 R1.0

Cover Photo © 2009 JupiterImages Corporation. All rights reserved - used with permission.

This book may not be reproduced, transmitted, or stored in whole or in part by any means, including graphic, electronic, or mechanical without the express written consent of the publisher except in the case of brief quotations embodied in critical articles and reviews.

Outskirts Press, Inc.
http://www.outskirtspress.com

ISBN: 978-1-4327-2376-7

Library of Congress Control Number: 2009921778

Outskirts Press and the "OP" logo are trademarks belonging to Outskirts Press, Inc.

PRINTED IN THE UNITED STATES OF AMERICA

Contents

Dedication	vii
Acknowledgements	xi
Transamerica Bicycle Trek Route	xiii
Typical Trip Tik	xvii
Trek Mechanical Services	xxi

Chapter One: **Washington State** — 1
- Day 1 Seattle to Skykomish
- Day 2 Skykomish to Wenatchee
- Day 3 Wenatchee to Coulee City
- Day 4 Coulee City to Spokane

Chapter Two: **Idaho** — 23
- Day 5 Spokane to Sandpoint

Chapter Three: **Montana** — 27
- Day 6 Sandpoint to Thompson Falls
- Day 7 Thompson Falls to Elmo
- Day 8 Elmo to West Glacier
- Day 9 Rest Day West Glacier
- Day 10 West Glacier to St Mary
- Day 11 St Mary to Shelby
- Day 12 Shelby to Havre
- Day 13 Havre to Malta
- Day 14 Malta to Ft Peck
- Day 15 Ft Peck to Poplar

Chapter Four:	**North Dakota**	63
	Day 16 Polar to Williston	
	Day 17 Rest Day Williston	
	Day 18 Williston to New Town	
	Day 19 New Town to Max	
	Day 20 Max to Harvey	
	Day 21 Harvey to Cooperstown	
	Day 22 Cooperstown to Moorhead	
Chapter Five:	**Minnesota**	79
	Day 23 Moorhead to Alexandria	
	Day 24 Alexandria to St Cloud	
	Day 25 Rest Day St Cloud	
	Day 26 St Cloud to Minneapolis	
	Day 27 Minneapolis to Wabasha	
Chapter Six:	**Wisconsin**	91
	Day 28 Wabasha to Sparta	
	Day 29 Sparta to Baraboo	
	Day 30 Baraboo to Lake Mills	
	Day 31 Lake Mills to Milwaukee	
	Day 32 Rest Day Milwaukee	
Chapter Seven:	**Indiana**	103
	Day 33 Milwaukee to Chicago	
	Day 34 Chicago to Valparaiso	
	Day 35 Valparaiso to Delphi	
	Day 36 Delphi to Indianapolis	
	Day 37 Indianapolis to Richmond	
Chapter Eight:	**Ohio**	129
	Day 38 Richmond to Columbus	
	Day 39 Columbus to Zanesville	
Chapter Nine:	**West Virginia**	135
	Day 40 Zanesville to Wheeling	
	Day 41 Rest Day Wheeling	

Chapter Ten:	**Pennsylvania**	141
	Day 42 Wheeling to Ohiopyle	
	Day 43 Ohiopyle to Bedford	
	Day 44 Bedford to Chambersburg	
	Day 45 Chambersburg to Lancaster	
Chapter Eleven:	**New Jersey**	153
	Day 46 Lancaster to Collingswood	
	Day 47 Collingswood to Atlantic City	
Epilogue		161

Dedication

This book is dedicated to my granddaughter Lindsey Louise Haight and my former boss and friend Stanley O. McNaughton

Lindsey Louise Haight

Lindsey was born on December 30 1988. After only four hours of life Lindsey was diagnosed with Trisomy 21, the most common form of Downs Syndrome.

In May of 1989 my daughter Sheri and Lindsey made the trip to Seattle, Washington for her brother's wedding. This was the last time I saw Lindsey. After returning home Lindsey became ill with a flu virus. She was treated at the medical facility on post and was transferred by ambulance to Duke University Hospital.

Between June and August 1989, Lindsey under went the first of three open heart surgeries to repair a hole in her heart. On August 25, 1989 after 61 days in a coma, Lindsey was taken off life support and allowed to pass away peacefully.

Lindsey was a fighter and my inspiration during the Trek. I thought of her often and I dedicate this book to her spirit.

Stanley O. McNaughton

I met Stanley O McNaughton, Pemco Financial Services President and CEO in November of 1982. I had applied for a position as Night Operations Manager. The company decided not to fill the position till the next year. Rather than just thanking me for applying and letting me leave, Stan checked with Human Resources to see what other positions might be available. He offered me a job in the Underwriting Department and I accepted. That was on November 1, 1982 and little did I know that I would stay there for the next

20 years. When I started PEMCO was a relatively small company. It always amazed me how Stan knew everyone's name's including family members. Stan had a fantastic ability to remember numbers also. Every Christmas we had a company meeting where Stan would give a rundown on the company's financial status. This included maybe 25-30 different statistics. He never had notes and had everything memorized. Stan had a concern for those disadvantaged through no fault of their own. Pemco Financial Services consistently donated a significant portion of its pre-tax income to many charities. I became involved with several organizations such as Hospice of Seattle, The American Lung Association and Junior Achievement. Stan never turned me down when I asked for support. I could tell many stories of his generosity but one particular story always comes to mind. I got a call from Stan one afternoon to come to his office, when I got there he told me that he had just heard about a new employee that was having some immediate problems feeding her children and paying bills. He told me to take his station wagon and fill it with groceries, take it to her house along with a check for $1,000. Needless to say a few tears were shed when I made the delivery. Everyone that knew Stan has one of these stories to tell. So back to the book and how Stan made my ride across America possible. In 1988 I was doing a lot of bicycle rides with The American Lung Association. I knew they did a ride from Seattle to Atlantic City, but it never entered my mind to attempt it. For one thing you had to take two months off work and you had to raise $5,000 in contributions. Maybe I could raise the money but I couldn't afford two months with no pay even if they would give me the time off. At that time one of my hobbies was making wild life pieces in ceramic bisque. I used a process called chalking. I don't remember how but Stan saw one of my eagles and asked if I would be interested in doing enough of them to give to the Board of Directors at Christmas. I agreed and Stan paid for all of the materials up front so I wouldn't have to use my own money. It took a lot of work but when they were ready I was invited to a Board meeting to present them. After that was over and as I was getting ready to leave one of the Board Members who I had mentioned the ride to one day at lunch called me back and

asked me to tell about the ride with the American Lung Association that I was interested in doing. I later found out that his daughter had done the ride a few years earlier. I told them what the ride was about, the length of time needed to be away from work and the fund raising requirement. I was asked a few more questions and then someone asked Stan what he thought. Stan looked at me for a few seconds and then said he thought I should do it. He said I could have two months off with pay and to come up to his office tomorrow and he would give me a check for $5,000. I was in shock when I left the room. That's how I got the #1 on my jersey. The next day I ran right over to the American Lung Association and turned in my money. Since I was first I got #1. They could not believe the generosity of PEMCO. I hadn't mentioned the ride to my boss so she wasn't exactly happy about me being gone for two months.

When Stan passed away on the morning of January 19, 1998 it was hard on everyone. It was so sudden that we were all in shock. Stan reached into many hearts. We were like family. I remember one of Stan's favorite saying. "If you see someone without a smile, give them yours." I dedicate this book to my boss, teacher and friend Stanley O. McNaughton

Acknowledgements

This book is not a solo effort, I am simply the facilitator. All of the 300 cyclists and 50 or more support staff that participated in this ride contributed. If not in writing then in spirit and support.

A special thank you to Trekker #280 Guy Smith who I feel wrote the best account of the Trek. His notes were excellent, his flow and passion came through. His wide range of experiences with a great variety of riders makes his contribution to this book invaluable.

I would be very remiss if I did not give a special acknowledgement and thanks to our two event managers, Dave Shaw and Gayle Delanty. In view of unforeseen events that transpired on our Trek, I am in awe of how Dave and Gayle dealt with the day to day problems and the tragedy of a death. I am sure that they both had their private moments of grief but to the group they were our rocks. With 300 completely different personalities everyday must have held a variety of challenges and problems. Not once in those 47 days did I see either of them falter. So Dave and Gayle on behalf of all the Trekkers you have our respect, admiration and love. Thank you very much for all you did.

Also a special thanks to four key staff people. Bill Glazier, Public Relations Coordinator, Rusty Burwell. Office Manager, Cassie Giddings, Logistics and Paul Clark, Communications.

Transamerica Bicycle Trek Route

JUNE 5 - JULY 21, 1989

DAY	LOCATION	MI	TOT	DAY	DATE
0	Seattle, WA	0	0	Mon	5 Jun
1	Skykomish, WA	70	70	Mon	5 Jun
2	Wenatchee, WA	68	138	Tue	6 Jun
3	Coulee City, WA	69	207	Wed	7 Jun
4	Spokane, WA	99	306	Thu	8 Jun
5	Sandpoint, ID	78	384	Fri	9 Jun
6	Thompson Falls, MT	89	473	Sat	10 Jun
7	Elmo, MT	73	546	Sun	11 Jun
8	West Glacier, MT	67	613	Mon	12 Jun
9	West Glacier, MT	0	613	Tue	13 Jun
10	St Mary, Mt	52	665	Wed	14 Jun
11	Shelby, MT	89	754	Thu	15 Jun

DAY	LOCATION	MI	TOT	DAY	DATE
12	Havre, MT	107	861	Fri	16 Jun
13	Malta, MT	91	952	Sat	17 Jun
14	Ft. Peck, MT	93	1045	Sun	18 Jun
15	Poplar, MT	69	1114	Mon	19 Jun
16	Williston, ND	79	1193	Tue	20 Jun
17	Williston, ND	0	1193	Wed	21 Jun
18	New Town, ND	75	1268	Thu	22 Jun
19	Max, ND	70	1338	Fri	23 Jun
20	Harvey, ND	77	1415	Sat	24 Jun
21	Cooperstown, ND	105	1520	Sun	25 Jun
22	Moorhead, ND	97	1617	Mon	26 Jun
23	Alexandria, MN	106	1723	Tue	27 Jun
24	St Cloud, MN	78	1801	Wed	28 Jun
25	St Cloud, MN	0	1801	Thu	29 Jun
26	Minneapolis, MN	80	1881	Fri	30 Jun
27	Wabasha, MN	86	1967	Sat	1 Jul
28	Sparta, WI	91	2058	Sun	2 Jul
29	Baraboo, WI	82	2140	Mon	3 Jul

DAY	LOCATION	MI	TOT	DAY	DATE
30	Lake Mills, WI	69	2209	Tue	4 Jul
31	Milwaukee, WI	54	2263	Wed	5 Jul
32	Milwaukee, WI	0	2263	Thu	6 Jul
33	Chicago, IL	89	2352	Fri	7 Jul
34	Valparaiso, IL	78	2430	Sat	8 Jul
35	Delphi, IN	80	2510	Sun	9 Jul
36	Indianapolis, IN	68	2578	Mon	10 Jul
37	Richmond, IN	85	2663	Tue	11 Jul
38	Columbus, OH	100	2763	Wed	12 Jul
39	Zanesville, OH	67	2830	Thu	13 Jul
40	Wheeling, WV	88	2918	Fri	14 Jul
41	Wheeling, WV	0	2918	Sat	15 Jul
42	Ohiopyle, PA	90	3008	Sun	16 Jul
43	Bedford, PA	76	3084	Mon	17 Jul
44	Chambersburg, PA	59	3143	Tue	18 Jul
45	Lancaster, PA	83	3226	Wed	19 Jul
46	Collingswood, NJ	74	3300	Thu	20 Jul
47	Atlantic City, NJ	63	3363	Fri	21 Jul

Trip Tik

NOTE: *This is the actual Trip Tik that we received for Day 1 of the Trek. The left-hand column (MI) is the mileage between landmarks, turns, junctions, and other points of interest. The right hand column (CUM) has the cumulative miles to that point. In smaller communities, cafes and groceries are noted. Larger towns usually have pharmacies, hardware and sporting goods stores. Etc., as well as food and these are noted by "full service". On the back of each trip tik page is a very basic map of the course with the route highlighted.*

TRIP TIK

| DAY 1 | Seattle - Skykomish 71 miles |
| 5 Jun | Monday |

Mi	Cum	
00	00	Pier 70 parking lot, Seattle waterfront, LEFTOnto Broad St, IMMEDIATE LEFT to Elliot
0.7	0.7	LEFT onto Western Ave.
1.2	1.9	BECOMES 15th Ave
1.2	3.1	Ballard Bridge, USE CENTER LANE
0.6	3.7	STEELE BRIDGE DECK, SLOW
2.5	6.2	BECOMES Holman Road
1.3	7.5	LEFT onto Greenwood. USE MIDDLE LANE. RIGHT TURN TURNS RIGHT ONLY
1.3	8.8	RIGHT onto 130th
0.5	9.3	CROSS Aurora Ave.
0.9	10.2	CROSS 1-5, bear right, becomes Roosevelt NE
0.4	10.6	BEAR LEFT onto 125th
1.1	11.7	LEFT onto Lake City Way, LEFT TURN LANE

xvii

2.6	14.3	ENTER Lake Forest Park
1.5	15.8	CROSS 68th Ave NE AVOID RIGHT TURN ONLY LANE
2.7	18.5	CROSS Intersection to Main St. AVOID RIGHT TURN ONLY LANE
0.1	18.6	RIGHT onto 102nd NE Cross Sammamish River
0.3	18.9	LEFT onto Riverside Drive
1.9	20.8	LEFT at stop sign onto NE 175th Street ENTER Woodinville RR Tracks
0.9	21.7	BECOMES Woodinville-Duvall Rd. Cross 140th Ave NE
1.3	23.0	LEFT onto 156th Ave NE
1.4	24.4	BECOMES 75th Ave NE
1.0	25.4	RIGHT onto 224th SE BECOMES Bostian Rd
1.4	26.8	Left onto Paradise Lake Rd, then IMMEDIATELY Onto Sr522
3.9	30.7	follow Snohomish River
2.6	33.3	STRAIGHT to follow SR522 DO NOT EXIT onto 164th St.
1.8	35.1	BEAR RIGHT then LEFT onto US 2 East. BOTH LANES TURN LEFT. END SR 522
0.2	35.3	RR Tracks. Enter Monroe Full Services

CHECKPOINT

7.1	42.4	ENTER Sultan Full Services
0.5	42.9	rest area on left next to the river.
0.7	43.6	City Park with picnic shelter on right. Café and food stores.
3.0	46.6	ENTER Startup. Cafes
2.0	48.6	ENTER Gold Bar Full Services City park on Right with picnic shelter
3.7	52.3	Zekes Café on right. Caboose
4.2	56.5	CROSS Skykomish River
0.3	56.8	ENTER Index. Café on left.
5.6	62.4	Store on right
0.7	63.1	Store on right

4.3	67.4	Money Creek Campground. Restrooms, water
2.8	70.2	Skykomish cafes, deli food store in town Across bridge
0.8	71.0	RIGHT onto gravel road opposite Beckler River Road to City Park.

DAY 1 = 71.0 Trip = 71.0

Lights off after 9:30 p.m.
Services: Deli, stores and cafes in town ½ mile from camp.

Mechanical Services

We had three mechanic's vans traveling with us across the country. The mechanic's were able to keep you going with good quality parts. Before we left Seattle we had to fill out a form telling about the type of bicycle we were riding so they would carry the proper parts. You were charged standard retail prices. You had to pay for parts and, if necessary, labor, when you picked up your bicycle. In most cases the labor was free.

For routine bicycle work, such as tightening brakes, changing tires, or making a saddle adjustment, you were issued a book of coupons. The coupons entitled you to this service free of charge. Once you used your coupons, you were charged a small labor charge for the service. The labor charge was donated to a fund to offset costs such as van maintenance, new tire pumps or bike stands.

It was not uncommon for these gentlemen to work all night to make sure that all the bikes were ready to be on the road first thing in the morning. They were also able to make some emergency requisitions of parts and bikes. We never asked them how they managed this they just did it. As you will find out in the book, they did some very creative things. A very special thanks to Craig, Jose and Duane.

Chapter 1

Day 1 Seattle Washington to Skykomish Washington 70 miles as remembered by Trekkers Marianne Brems #49, Guy Smith #280, Virgil Kemp #154, Nancy Eiselt #6, and Mike Mitchell #1

NOTE: *The first time that a new Trekker appears it will be preceded by their biography which will tell what they were doing in 1989 and why they went on the Trek.*

So we are off and pedaling. Sit back and enjoy this adventure as seen through the eyes of those that experienced it. At the end I hope you will feel like you were on the ride with us.

BIO NANCY EISELT #6

In June of 1989, I was 30 years old, had been married nearly 5 years, and had been a consultant with Andersen Consulting in Seattle for 3 years. I was feeling some professional restlessness and uncertainty at the time. I think my biggest reason for riding Trek was probably the need to do something audacious as I entered my 30's.

(Nancy Eiselt #6) Today was a day of intense emotion All the nervous energy, excitement, anxiety and sadness I've felt about making this trip were with me this morning as I crawled out of bed. It was hard to imagine that I wouldn't be crawling back into bed with my husband for almost 7 weeks. And then the thought of,"Can I make it"? "Will I have an accident?" "Will Dan be OK?" and about a million others thoughts started fogging my mind. I went through the motions all morning not really attached to what was occurring, and before I knew it I was in the lineup of cyclists moving slowly toward the departure point."

BIO MARIANNE BREMS #49 In 1989 I was teaching English as a Second Language in Adult Education and I was about to start my first ESL textbook. As a matter of fact, the soon to be publisher of my book wanted me to submit a very specific sample of my work, the parameters of which were not ready before I left on Trek so I said "Send them to my first mail stop". So the first rest day we had I looked over the assignment and began planning my sample. I submitted my text and in August. I found out I got the contract for the book. My main reason for going on Trek was to get a break from my daily life, I had just turned 40 and wanted a physical challenge to show I still had life left in me (seems strange now that I am not far from 60), and I had been a competitive swimmer for more than 20 years, was tired of competition and I wanted a new sport that I would never compete in.

(Marianne Brems #49) It was fascinating to see how everyone packed. Some brought huge, unwieldy packs, other's brought one's barely big enough for a patch kit.

My throat tightened and I felt tears in my eyes repeatedly throughout the early morning until we were out of Seattle. It truly is a momentous event of what can seem like major proportions. I guess it's in my voice, I got a pledge today. Today was also a day of adjustment's. A helmet adjustment, a cycle computer adjustment and an attitude adjustment.

BIO MIKE MITCHELL TREKKER #1

In 1989 I was working in the insurance industry with a great company, PEMCO Financial Services. Through my company I was involved in several charitable organizations such as Hospice, Junior Achievement, Northwest Harvest and the American Lung Association.(ALA)It was my association with the ALA that ultimately got me on the Trek.That and the fact that my company helped me with the fund raising requirement and gave me the time off. Up to that point I had never ridden further than 30 miles in one day. I had some definite training challenges ahead of me. Thanks to a small hard core cycling group within the company the training was fun and hard. Like most of the people that left Seattle, I could have been better prepared.

(**Mike Mitchell#1**) I think for many of us day one was sort of a blur. We had been training and fund raising for so long that it was hard to believe that we were about to head out on the road. I'm sure that we all anticipated some injuries, a lot of pain and soreness but I don't think death ever entered our minds. Nevertheless all 300 of us representing 42 states and four countries headed out from Seattle with great expectations of a lot of fun, hard work and great memories. These would all be fulfilled, but little did we realize the depth with which we would bond. For 20 years this has been my family. To this day I would help anyone of these people solely on the basis of the Trek. For me the first day was pretty much a solo day. I was very nervous about the large group riding together. I had unpleasant memories of accidents on some of the previous large rides I had been on. Primarily the Seattle to Portland Ride. So on this first day I found myself riding alone on streets that I was very familiar with. A great deal of my training had been on these very roads. The Burke Gillman trail was my number one training ride. So I was riding with ease even as we hit the first slow climbs, I felt good. About that time my legs started to burn and I knew even with all of my training I was still going to need more conditioning for what lay ahead. I made it to Skykomish, a 70 mile ride in the middle of the afternoon. I headed for the gear truck and my duffel bag. We were allocated a cubicle 15X15X36. The bag had to include your tent, your sleeping bag and all your clothing. The cubicles were stacked four high and the lucky people got the bottom shelves so they didn't have to go up a ladder and carrying everything down. Having #1 I was sure I would be on the bottom only to find out the first time I loaded that they had started from the top down. I went about setting up my tent for the first time. In a week or so this would become something that you could do in your sleep. I checked out the showers and the bathrooms and was totally amazed by how clean everything was, how the toilets didn't stink and was told that I could shower in hot water for as long as I wanted. You talk about spoiled. Out first meal (Mexican food) was outstanding as were almost every meal. It's seems like everyone tried to outdo the last group. We owe a great deal of gratitude to all of the groups across America that went out of there way to see to our needs. It was amazing to see the camp go up for the first time and to really realize that we were a city on wheels. I didn't sleep great that first night but my normal sleep pattern is only about five hours and this would be about my norm on the Trek.

BIO GUY SMITH TREKKER #280

The year 1989 was a roller coaster ride. In January, I was on my way up, you know, the colossal initial climb just before the first plunge. I had just retired from 22 years in the US Navy. While trying to get my bearings on what to do with the rest of my life. I was teaching college part-time in Denver and living with my brother's family in secluded Morrison, CO, in the foothills of the Rockies. I had connected with a former girlfriend, an Air Force doc who had been transferred to Korea. She was considerable younger than me, but our correspondence was warming rapidly, and she wanted me to come to Korea to be with her. What a wonderful opportunity! I planned to spend the entire summer there, getting to know my doc better and exploring South Korea, famous for exotic food, varied architecture and legendary shopping. Best of all, I would buy a new bicycle and explore the country on my favorite mode of transportation. Things were getting even better in early spring, my doc had a business trip to St Louis and she invited me to come visit there.

Disaster! On our second day together, I tossed all my things into a suitcase, hurriedly left the hotel and spent the night at the airport. I arrived in Denver very early the next morning, too inconvenient to call my brother, so I walked around the airport for several hours trying to work out what to do with my summer, now that Korea was irrelevant. The roller coaster had come crashing down. I vaguely remembered a mailing that I had gotten about a bicycle ride across America, and I pondered the idea while my sister-in-law came to rescue me. Recognizing my distress; she drove me straight to a bicycle store in Boulder where I bought a new bicycle that could handle the rigors of a cross county trek. The roller coaster was starting to soar skyward again. I began my training the very next day with a ride along the famous "hogback" from Boulder to Morrison.

The roller coaster began another nose-dive when I realized I had to raise a minimum of $5,000 in less than two months. I didn't even know where to begin. My brother Pete, sent me soaring into the fund-raising adventure with an on the spot check for $500. It was my first day of fundraising - I already had 10% of my goal. I created a flyer about the Trans America adventure and began writing personal notes to everybody that I had ever know - including a certain doctor in Korea. In my flyer, I promised to send a postcard to everyone who sponsored me, and, if sponsors paid a penny a mile ($34) I would send them a copy of my trip report after the Trek. One of these flyers went to a couple in Maryland, former students from my Navy days. They eagerly sponsored me and even persuaded one of their co-workers to sponsor their friend who would ride a bicycle across America. This co-worker and her daughter wrote a check for $34, and unbeknownst to either of us, we had boarded another roller coaster ride. That thirty four dollar check is now framed and has a place of honor on the wall of our bedroom. That is another story- part of the sequel to Trans America 1989. There were many remarkable stories of people who generously responded to my appeal for the American Lung Association; and I arrived in Seattle on June 5, 1989 with $2.66 pledge for every mile I would ride. With steep mountains, flat plains, narrow valleys and rolling hills before me; my bicycle was ready for the roller coaster ride of Trans America 1989.

(Guy Smith #280) On day one we all gathered in the AAA parking lot behind the hotel for our first breakfast together. After stowing our tents and equipment in the gear truck, a tandem tractor trailer rig, one of the vehicles that would accompany us on the road, we assembled on Pier 70 of the Seattle waterfront for the formal start. The pier was bursting with energy. Riders dipped their rear wheels into the Puget Sound a ceremony that would be concluded weeks later when the front wheel was dipped into the Atlantic Ocean.

Sunrise 47

Photos farewells, and 300 bicyclist pedaling through an archway of red, white, and blue balloons preceded by an escort - on bicycles, of course. Over the Ballard Bridge and through the Seattle streets we rode, hooting and hollering while people waved and cheered from cars and houses. I remember how unreal it felt: I was thinking of the 3363 miles of rode ahead, just how much fun it was at that spectacular moment. We rode as a mass for about ten miles, then spread out to normal riding when the city faded into beautiful hilly suburbs with shade trees and highways with wide shoulders. Later we would reminisce about the great roads in the state of Washington, the best ones on the trip. I rode with several different people that day, but mostly with Karin from Seattle who had trained on these roads and acted as my tour guide. In Woodinville I rode over a small rock and got my first flat tire of the trip. I had been plagued with flat tires on my training rides and was disappointed that the jinx was still with me. Our route took us along the Skykomish River, churning and cascading over rocks, inviting us to cool off. We were in the Cascade mountain range around midday, but our route went through the canyon and avoided any major climbs for the first day. With 71 miles under our belt the Skykomish campground was a welcome sight and I was exuberant. I pitched my tent among tall pine trees and set out to meet new friends throughout the evening. Supper and breakfast were provided for us every day; the food was excellent and really plentiful appetites were enormous on the Trek with a reported 6000 calories consumed daily by each Trekker.

BIO VIRGIL KEMP #154

While on the 87 TA ride going thru Montana I had a toothache. The next morning the sag took me to a dentist; it turned into a root canal. When the dentist finished with me I was behind the time line so the sag had to drive me 50 miles to catch up. After I finished the 87 TA I felt cheated because I missed 50 miles and I always rode no matter how I felt (sick, tired, further tooth problems whatever!!) I wanted to ride every mile of TA no excuses. I did that in 89.

(**Virgil Kemp #154**) I think one of the hardest days for me was the first day; esp; being from an area without mountains to train on.Because we were climbing a mountain the first day. The hills we have around Chicago I could always muscle up so I thought I was good to go. I did eventually learn to grind them out. And at 190 lbs. that's what it takes.

Day 2 Skykomish Washington to Wenatchee Washington 68 miles as remembered by Trekkers Mike Mitchell #1, Guy Smith #280, Mary Fleming #27, Sandy Kielmeyer Fredric #202, Ellen Lowe #42 and Marianne Brems #49

BIO SANDY KIELMEYER FREDRIC #202

In the fall of 1988 I was a new touring cyclist, in a new city (Seattle) and in a new profession (Secondary Education). I'd always been active in other sports and interested in cycling but didn't have a family that wanted to participate so it always slid to the back burner - now the opportunity was there so I climbed on my dated, dusty Camipani, after replacing cracked, flat tires and oiling the chain. A few weeks later, on a typically rainy evening I popped in to a bicycle shop not realizing I was covered in mud (no fender and traffic). A friendly stranger smiled and said "You look like a serious biker". I glanced in a shop mirror and quickly grabbed a tissue to wipe some of the mud off my face, not to mention the smeared black mascara creating a bit of a gothic look - some of my students at school would appreciate! We talked a few minutes and he offered to take me to the Burke-Gilman Trail out in the valley to enjoy some distance riding in a kinder environment. He glanced at my bike again and was polite not to comment on the 20 year antique. I actually thought it was a nice bike.

After meeting him for a couple of bike rides I was huffing and puffing to do 20 miles and he kept having to wait so I could catch up, he mentioned that If I had a different bike I might do better. I told him I had just relocated and money was tight. He said he knew a married couple that had purchased great new bikes 6 years ago and then decided the sport wasn't for them. He felt he could get me the low miles, like new, Trek bike - for $300 which included the thick dust. Yikes - seemed like a huge amount. He was sure it would be a perfect fit, he was right and I bought it on the spot.

A couple of months later we were out riding and had stopped to rest, probably because I needed to, when we ran into a friend of his (Jerry) who had completed Trans America the year before. I was in awe of his accomplishment. My friend turned to me and suggested that I ought to do the Trek, he said he couldn't get away from work but I could because of summer break. I really looked at him as if he were nuts and said I could never do that. It seemed like he was just teasing, but I saw quickly that he really meant it. We said good bye and finished our ride but, looking back, the seed had been planted in my sub-conscious.

Later that December (by chance), I happened to catch the local TV coverage of the Trek taking off from Seattle (probably footage of the year before.) and, not knowing one other soul that was going - I called the ALA and signed up. I then spent the next half year training and raising pledges. I didn't yet really have the confidence to believe I could do it, so decided the test for me would be a solo journey from my home in Kirkland WA to Wenatchee WA over Stevens pass in one day on my spring break. I figured if I could do that I wouldn't embarrass myself by having signed up for a bite that was to big for me to chew. Nobody but me would know.

You can't bike on I-405 so my sister dropped me off just after the Woodinville exit, of course in an unexpected heavy rain. She informed me that I was crazy and should cancel. I wrapped my feet, hands and helmet in cheap plastic bags and waved goodbye heading up towards Monroe. About 30 miles out and just when the bags were disintegrating the rain stopped and I pulled over to re-assess. I wasn't cold - all was good. It was exhilarating, challenging and scary in parts where the highway was narrow. In long, isolated spots I wondered at my judgment for safety and then diverted my mind, managed a quick prayer and rode on. I was encouraged about 50 miles out, when feeling my muscles straining as the grade increased and feeling lonely, I rode by a bunch of men working construction who hooted and hollered cheering me on thanks guys, I needed that.

Finally reaching the top of the pass (where there was a pay

phone - no cell then) I called my kids who lived in Wenatchee so they wouldn't worry. Immediately my son said "Mom stay right there and we'll come get you, you must be exhausted." No" I said, stunned," I'm on a high" - I just did the up hill and now I'm going to enjoy the downhill". I was worried about beating the dark when I was about 25 miles out West of Wenatchee. I was slowing down to much but determined. It was 9:20 p.m. and almost dark when I crossed the new bridge to East Wenatchee and was about 8 blocks from my daughters house. In the very dim light I caught sight of my 5 year old granddaughter pedaling her bike to meet me, my eyes moistened with joy- I did it! It had taken me way too many hours on the seat of my bike (13.5 hrs) but I had managed 142 miles alone over Stevens - nothing could stop me now!

(Sandy Kielmeyer Fredric #202) Today we were headed over Steven's Pass, It seemed more grueling than when I did it alone because I felt the pressure to keep up, to at least be in the middle half. I guess - to prove myself. What kept me going was a little bakery in Leavenworth - that was my carrot for the day. I kept focusing on the little treat/reward waiting for me - silly but it was working, keeping my mind off the steep grade that was punishing my muscles. I loved sweets and had frequented the place during the 20 years I resided in Wenatchee.

I don't remember where I was exactly but I'll never forget when the SAG vehicle came by and said we had to detour from Leavenworth thru Plains. That was a big punch in my gut for me. Not only would I miss the bakery but I had driven that route a couple of times and remembered a very steep grade on a lousy rode. Yikes! Now the out of state Trekkers didn't know this but some of the Washington group did. I remember one (unknown to me) guy I rode with a short distance on the steepest part - his face was bright red and he was soaking wet and I hoped he didn't have a stroke. I asked if he was okay, and he said yes. In fact his concern turned to me as he reminded me to pace myself - I must have looked desperate to get over the top. Anyway it ended well and my son's met me in Wenatchee where we camped, I was darn happy I had made it this far.

(Mike Mitchell #1) I remember it was really cold when I got out of my tent that first morning. Could it be because I was up before sunrise? I was going to have to work on staying in the sleeping bag longer. I was even too early for breakfast. I tried to be as quite as possible breaking down my tent and packing but I could hear a few zippers starting to open. This was one way to know when the camp was waking up. I stowed my bag by the gear truck and as dawn arrived I headed out. I knew that Steven's pass lay ahead (4,000 feet) and I was planning a slow climb in Granny gear. I was very cautious with the knees and made sure to spin in the morning. About a half hour into my ride I got off and stretched for about ten minutes. This became my routine and served me well. I never had any knee problems on the entire ride. Many of us were fortunate to make friends with a black bear that day. Some were even silly enough to try to get close for a picture.

He or she was a friendly thing and set on a rock and watched us for a long time. The climb went well and as I came around the last bend in the road I could see the summit. I had enough climb for one day. On the backside I had just started down the steep grade when my chain popped off. I was very fortunate that it didn't go into my spokes and I was able to stop safely and put it back on. Made some adjustments in the evening so it wouldn't happen again. The highlight of the day for me was going through Leavenworth. This is where I now live and my daughter, son-in-law and three grandsons have a home just as you get into town. It is a great place to live and is beautiful. A lot of the Trekkers hit the Dairy Queen and started a trend for the next 45 days. Stop at every Dairy Queen. I made it to the Wenatchee River County Park with no problem and again enjoyed seeing tent city come to life. I then headed to the shower truck and was still amazed that I could stay in there as long as I wanted and the hot water never ran out.

I happened to put my bike by my tent so I could clean it. Most of the other Trekkers put their bikes against a fence, in the morning they woke up to find 20-30 slugs on each bike. How gross was that. It was funny to some of us but not to the one's that had to clean their bikes. That was the first of a thousand funny things to add to the memory bank. Dinner was great but I still walked across the highway later to get a milkshake before bed. Early to bed and I hoped to sleep longer.

(**Guy Smith #280**) It was gloomy and overcast as the second day began. It took me a long time to break camp, no routine had been worked out yet. The highlight of the day
was the climb to Steven's pass in a dense fog. A black bear set along side the road watching the parade of bikes and providing a real photo opportunity. East of Steven's pass, just beyond the ski area which was shrouded in mist, the weather cleared rapidly and I enjoyed my first downhill ride averaging 43 miles per hour. I met Lori and Michelle grad students from the San Francisco Bay area. Together we toured Leavenworth, a dramatic Bavarian town in the mountains. We enjoyed ice cram in a German steam train, and snoozed in the town park. We completed the journey to the Wenatchee River County Park, right beside the river, our home for the evening. Muscles were beginning to feel strained, but there was a real sense of accomplishment, leaving our first big mountain range behind - the Cascades. Ahead lay the Eastern Washington desert.

BIO MARY FLEMING #27

In 1989 I was working in a high stress job with the local county government. I managed a group of Land Use Planners for the Community Development Department and had several years to go before retirement was even a possibility. I loved my job but it was stressful.

In 1988 our local paper ran a series of articles about some local people that were traveling across the United States on a bike. Having done some casual bike touring I thought this trip sounded like a great opportunity to do it at a relatively low cost. I wasn't sure if I would be able to raise the $5,000 required but decided it was worth a try. Well I was very fortunate and raised $16,000 from friends, family and the local development community.

(**Mary Fleming #27**) At 5:00 a.m. we all became very much aware of the fact that our campground was within a short distance of the railroad tracks.

Getting up and moving out early is going to be very important for awhile. I need to maximize the time available for travel and I need to avoid as much heat as possible. Later when I'm stronger (wishful thinking) it won't be as critical.

It was overcast this morning and quite cool. Our outdoor breakfast consisted of either corn flakes or apple jacks, a large sweet roll, a piece of orange, grapefruit and cantaloupe, a hard boiled egg (hot) and a piece of melba toast. Orange juice and coffee were also available.

The ride from Skykomish to Steven's Pass was 16 miles long with an elevation gain of 3,000 feet. The majority of it occurring in the last 5 miles or so. We got lots of support at times like the water vans. Even if you don't need water it provides a good place to stop and rest.

I have a new computer on my bike that measures current speed, average speed, total mileage and cadence. I really appreciate the trip distance feature on the more difficult rides because I can do a mental countdown on remaining miles. Psychologically that number in my head that keeps going down is more of an incentive to keep moving than the one displayed on the computer that keeps going up.

The ride down from Stevens Pass was great. Suddenly we came out of the clouds and could see the mountains with their left over snow seeming to have settled in for the summer. The ride was several miles of coasting down the hill with nothing but the sound of the wind and of the tires humming across the pavement in our ears.

On the way up to Steven's Pass we saw a black bear. He seemed to want to cross the road but all of those bikers standing there watching him appeared to intimidate him and he retreated up the hill to sit behind a tree until the crowd thinned. When it was down to me and one other person he decided to brave it and came on down. Even though logically I was certain that he would not attack anyone that was not threatening him I decided that it was time to continue the ride shortly before he reached the road.

My timing was better today and I found a shady spot for the tent and a shower with no line. We had a short instructional period with the bicycle mechanic to discuss the issue of determining proper air pressure for tires. By then it was time for dinner which consisted of green salad, rice with spaghetti sauce and bread, cake and fruit were available for dessert.

BIO ELLEN LOWE #42

In 1989 I was 42 years old and working for Charles W Carter Company in Los Angeles California as a Accounts Receiving/Credit Collection Manager. I was married with three daughters, Shelley age 21, Lisa age 16 and Robyn age 9. I saw Trek as the adventure of a lifetime with the opportunity to see the country up close and personal from the seat of a bicycle while raising money for a great cause. What a great chance to spend quality time with my 21 year old daughter, Shelley, before she finished college and moved on to marriage and a family of her own. We were the only Mother-Daughter team on the Trek.

(Ellen Lowe #42) I remember coming out of the Bavarian town of Leavenworth, WA, to find a grueling climb consisting of numerous switchbacks. After a long, slow climb to the top, I stopped to catch my breath and spotted a rider at the bottom, who I thought was my daughter, Shelley. I cheered and hollered words of encouragement and support as she struggled up the hill. When this rider finally reached the top, she stopped to give me a huge hug plus thanks for the many cheers, it wasn't Shelley after all, this is where I first met Beth Grabhorn #50.

(Marianne Brems #49) I've now gotten compliments on my sox, my earrings, and my frame (bicycle frame).Someone did say I looked strong after he complimented me on my shorts.

Today was a day of snow and a day of 90 degree heat. A day of fog like pea soup and a day of no shirt.A flat tire the first on my Klein.

The tents are as close together as houses in California.A day of sharing with Elaine.A day most of all different from the first. Theresa was thrilled that I called. She describes how moments after all of us left the hotel it was again just a normal hotel.

Sunrise 47

Day 3 Wenatchee Washington to Coulee City Washington 69 miles as remembered by Trekkers Mike Mitchell #1, Guy Smith #280, Mary Fleming #28, Ellen Lowe #42 and Marianne Brems #49

NOTE: *We were often asked how much equipment we were allowed to bring and what did it include? You needed a variety of clothing, of course comfortable riding clothes, both long and short sleeve shirts and pants, personal bathroom items, waterproof tent, sleeping bag and a ground cover. That's not to say that there were not some unusual things brought. One couple had a full set up for espresso Coffee every morning. One couple had a full size blow up bed to go inside their tent. There were of course an assortment of radios and other electronic devices.*

(Mike Mitchell #1) My memory of today is that it was long and hot. Although it was only a 69 miles it seemed longer. We climbed 8 miles up Pine Canyon onto the plateau of Central Washington. At checkpoint I stopped at the Douglas General Store and had a great ice cream cone before getting back in the saddle. When we got to the High School at Coulee City I was ready to put up my tent and look for shade or better air conditioning. A short walk away was a great drive-in done in the 50's style. Great hamburgers, fries and shakes. Went back and chilled out in the gym and a couple of us walked down to a Laundromat and did some clothes. Several Trekkers chose to head to the community park and try to rest in the shade. Dinner was great and the night was humid.

(Guy Smith #280) Today I rode with Wendy from Colorado and her new friend Allison from Vermont. Wendy and I met at a pre-trek meeting in Colorado and did two training rides together. That conditioning came in handy on this hot, dry day up steep barren mountain slopes. At a snack stop in Waterville I met 6 year old Shannon Patrick who watched our bikes for a quarter. The mid day check point, Douglas was a typical tiny town in rural America, the Douglas General Store was it. In the afternoon I biked with Marty a sculptor from Atlanta, who loved to stop and chat with farmers in the fields and to meet the local people. We descended into Moses Coulee which is like a huge dry river bed. But at the end of the fun descent it was stifling hot, a great incentive to climb the other side to the plateau above. As soon as I set up my tent in the Coulee City Campground I enjoyed a refreshing swim in the Banks Lake. The huge reservoir created by the grand Coulee Dam. That night, vegetarian lasagna at the local high school was a big hit.

(Mary Fleming #28) What a miserable day! It started out well Wenatchee is located in a pretty green valley with the Columbia river flowing through it. We followed the river for 18 miles which was quite nice. The hills there are primarily sagebrush, but the valley is green and attractive.

The day was very hot again (upper 80's - low 90's) At Orondo we left the river and climbed up a canyon to the central state plateau, 8 miles distance and about 1500 feet higher. There were virtually no trees from that point on up the canyon.

At the top of the climb was a pleasant little town called Waterville. The people there were very friendly and full of questions regarding the trip. The school children were having a "last day of school" picnic in the park. One women brought her class over to ask questions and some other young girls stopped by to talk.

After Watterville the terrain was gently rolling agricultural land with occasional houses to be seen from the road. My plan to stop every 10 or 15 miles just did not work. It was much to hot to just sit in the sun. I pretty much kept moving with a brief stop when it just got to difficult. I seem to recover pretty quickly but just don't last long in the heat. I was really dragging when I got into camp. I am just exhausted but I want to go and make a phone call. Tomorrow is a 99 mile day. That should be interesting.

(Ellen Lowe #42) I remember the Douglas General Store in Douglas WA opening on Sunday exclusively so we could get snacks before heading across the "grand canyon" desert to Coulee City. The proprietor had stocked extra supplies and was amazed as he rang up sales non stop all morning long. Undoubtedly more revenue in one day than he typically experienced in a week. He soon found out that 300 hungry Trekkers plus the staff can spend a lot of $$$$'s.

(Marianne Brems #49) Today was a day of heat and some sunburn and further adjustments. I've been wearing my cycling shoes for 5 years with the laces too tight.

I bought shorts for 25 cents, 27 cents including tax at the Waterville thrift store. The money goes to support the museum. The town will be 100 years old tomorrow and their having a celebration. Clarice Besel who sold me the shorts gave me a $5.00 pledge. Mrs. Thompson in Coulee City doesn't drink beer and thinks you've got everything you need right in Coulee City (population 500)

Day 4 Coulee City Washington to Spokane Washington 99 miles as remembered by Trekkers Mike Mitchell #1, Guy Smith #280, Mary Fleming #27, Karin Allen #29 and Marianne Brems #49

NOTE: Shelley Lowe #34 and Ellen Lowe #42 were the only mother-daughter team on the Trek.

(**Mike Mitchell #1**)Up early again. Our first century of the trip and hot. Made sure both of my water bottles were filled and knew I would have to stop at every opportunity and replenish them. I decided to break the day into three thirty mile rides instead of thinking about the 100 miles. Mentally I think this helped. It didn't hurt that I was able to find my favorite (root beer float) twice during the day. The miles drifted by and I was happy to see the campus of Gonzaga University. Was looking forward to sleeping in a nice bed. Good dinner in the cafeteria and slept okay even though it was very humid.

(**Guy Smith #280**) Today was the first really big challenge of the Trek, our first century, 102 miles to Spokane. I started early, on the road by 6:30 having already eaten breakfast and broken down my camp, a morning routine which was already a habit. After an extensive detour, we rejoined US highway 2, the route which would take us more than 1/3 of the way across the US. I met Cam and Nancy from Alaska and we joined forces, reminding each other every few minutes to drink water. It was hard to keep ahead of dehydration and exhaustion. In the small town of Reardan I completely ran out of energy with 27 miles still to go.

After lots to drink and a nap right on the sidewalk of the town I summoned up enough strength to go on. Still I was shaky when we arrived at Gonzaga University in Spokane and really appreciated sleeping in a bed in the college dorm. I was proud of my accomplishment, I had completed long bike trips before, but this was my first official century.

BIO KARIN (VAN DER VELDEN) ALLEN #29

In the mid 80's I was working for a Seattle advertising agency (Sharp Hartwig). One of my accounts was the American Lung Association. I worked with Tim Kneeland to develop promotional materials for the Tri-Island Trek, a three day ALA fund raiser. In 1988 I was offered a position working out of Seattle for San Francisco based Foote, Cone & Belding on their Holland America business. When FCB decided to close the Seattle office in February of 1989, I was offered a transfer to San Francisco which I refused, but agreed to continue to work through April based out of another ad agency to transition the account. I then took the three month severance package they offered me. Having recently broken up with my boyfriend and now without a job, I made plans to take a month long solo trip to Europe in April and then spend a week in Cancun with two friends at Club Med. It was after those plans were finalized that Tim Kneeland suggested I go on the Trans America Bicycle Trek. There were three major problems. (1) I had only been on a bicycle three days in the last ten years (2) I was going to be gone five weeks in Europe and Mexico, leaving me only four weeks to get organized between the time I returned from my trips and when I would have to leave for Trek (3) I had to raise $5,000 in donations before the Trek started. Somehow I managed to get in a little training, make preparations, and raise the necessary money.

(Karin Allen #29) After riding our first century of the trip, I hobbled into the cafeteria at Gonzaga University and found myself near tears. I was so incredibly sore, so incredibly tired, and we were only on day 4 of 47. How in the world was I going to make it across the country? I sent a letter to my boy friend (we had broken up for several months but had 'sort of' gotten back together before the Trek) bitterly complaining of how hard this was and how miserable I felt. I wanted to go home.

(Marianne Brems #49) Sun and sore muscles are the theme of the day. I drafted with the Marines for 20 miles and made tremendous mileage, but I find a subtle (if that makes sense) kick butt attitude. I rode with Bonnie after lunch. That was I would say heart warming. The man at the Chevron station gave us lolly pops to get us into Spokane. Moments after, an elderly man honked crazily at us, and then pulled sharply over in front of us and blocked the whole bike lane. He jumped out of his car and got right up in Bonnie's face and said "Do you have an objection to someone honking at you?" She said "no". He said "then why did you give me the finger?" She said "I didn't I was just waving" "You went over the road line" he said and "I didn't want to hit you".

(Mary Fleming #27) Today was supposed to be the first chance to do a century (100 miles). I got up with the sun, was packed and had breakfast by 6 a.m. I felt extremely tired from yesterday and am beginning to feel the physical pressure. My bottom is getting very sore. I bought a Spenco saddle pad to help with that problem and it seems to be an improvement. They also keep a large supply of "Bag Balm" which, if applied to the appropriate locations, is supposed to help. They say that this concoction is used to soften the udders of cows. Why they want them softer I don't know.

My legs are getting sore and tired which is to be expected. We had a short seminar last night on the value of stretching and were given a handout on cycling stretches. They say not to do stretching until you have had a chance to warm up with some riding. I am hoping that another day or two on the bike my legs will start to get better. Maybe I should schedule a massage from our support massage staff.

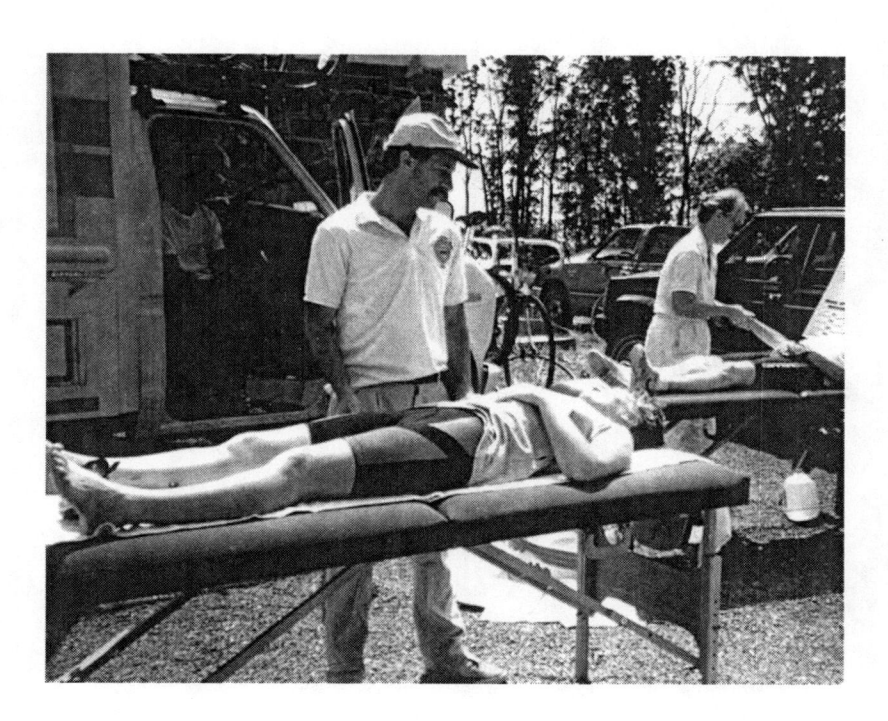

I began to have a problem with my hands yesterday and today. I keep shifting them around to keep them from cramping but nothing feels comfortable for long. Some of our riders have a bar protruding forward from the handlebars so that they can rest on their elbows and forearms. Maybe that is a good idea. I think I may have gotten my seat a little high when I was trying to take some of the pressure off my knees. Tomorrow I will lower it a little.

The biggest problem for me right now is the heat. I need to locate a long sleeve white shirt to keep the sun off. I am wearing lots of sun block but my skin is still reacting. I also have to keep reminding myself to drink lots of water. They recommend one quart per hour. Tomorrow I will focus on that goal and take along one container of Gatorade.

Chapter 2

Day 5 Spokane Washington to Sandpoint Idaho 78 miles as remembered by Trekkers Guy Smith #280, Mary Fleming #27, Sandy Kielmeyer Fredric #202, Ellen Lowe #42 and Marianne Brems #49

NOTE: *Trekkers came from all parts of the country and are of many different backgrounds. 55% were men and 45% women. The average age was 34, although many people in their 60's have participated. The oldest has been 72.*

(Guy Smith #280) Shortly outside Spokane the scenery changed drastically from hot, dry desert and irrigated fields to thick hilly woods with the fresh smell of pines filling the air. I rode with Ellen, another rider from Team Alaska who was very strong and set a challenging pace. In Newport, the last town in Washington, we mingled with the "Bike America" group, another cross-country Trek. Checkpoint activates for the day included an impromptu water pistol and water balloon fight. Riding into Idaho was a big milestone, completing our trip across Washington. Idaho roads were narrow and rough, torn up by the big logging trucks that thundered past and kept us hugging the roads edge. At Priest River, a gorgeous town along the Pend Oreille River, I stuffed myself at lunch time with clam chowder, baked Idaho potatoes, a sandwich and a chocolate malt. My body refused to move. My legs felt like cement until I had digested some of that food. It was an agonizing trip up and down steep hills to Sandpoint, our overnight stop along the lake. All day long it had threatened to rain, and it came down in buckets, shortly after I arrived in camp. Supper was another highlight - baked potatoes with all kinds of wonderful fillings served by kids from a local church.

(Mary Fleming #28) I woke up feeling much more energetic than yesterday. I decided to wear tights all day to keep the sun off my legs. I borrowed a long sleeve white shirt also. I am getting a rash on my legs in spite of the sun block. I'm not quite sure what that is all about.

Breakfast was oatmeal, pancakes, eggs, hash browns and sausages, cold cereal, apples, oranges, fruit juices, coffee and milk were also available.

The ride from Spokane to Sand Point was lovely. It is a beautiful area, rolling hills, lots of trees and water. No difficult terrain, though once we got into Idaho the traffic seemed to increase and the road was not as well maintained. There was a lot of sand and debris on the shoulder area and at the end (20 miles or so) there was virtually no shoulder and many logging trucks.

Sand Point is a very nice town. There is a river flowing through town and a shopping area built on a bridge out over the water. The shops are much more sophisticated than in many areas we have been through. It could be that this is a retail or resort center for the area.

The Boy Scouts did dinner for us. Baked potatoes, (we are in Idaho now) with either chili cheese or stroganoff over them. Salad and dessert. The kids were serving the drinks and dessert and seemed to be enjoying it.

Arrangements have been made to house us in a motel at six to a room, which seemed a little strange to me when I heard about it. When I discovered that the rooms had two double beds and that I was the sixth person, I decided I would prefer to just put up the tent and sleep there, which was one of our options. They had asked us to register for a room even if we intended to camp so that they would have access to showers and other facilities. Unfortunately when I went to take a shower there was no hot water and all of the towels, except for one hand towel had been used.

Though none of this seemed to be a major problem, just awkward, I thought it was the first instance of poor planning on their part.

I put my borrowed tent up and because it was getting overcast I put the rain fly on. It didn't seem quite right because the rain fly was in contact with the tent, which I thought was not suppose to happen. I decided to make a trip to the store and then came back and adjust it further. Unfortunately, while I was gone it poured and when I got back it was very wet inside. What to do now? Everything is wet, the room I'm registered into is crowded and there would be no way to dry my wet gear. I decided to rent a room of my own and spread out and get everything dry. The weather report says we may have showers tomorrow. I am going to have to dry out the tent and figure out how to keep it dry.

(Sandy Kielmeyer Fredric #202) Months prior when I was in serious training, my right knee (an old ski injury) started acting up. In fact both knees hurt so much I'd have to stop riding after about 35 miles - it was so painful to bend them and make the rotation. My doctor suggested surgery. I said no way as I wouldn't heal in time to go on the Trek. I heard about a sports medicine doctor who was an avid biker so I went to see him. He said the problem was that I simply didn't have enough muscle to support the stress and protect my knees. He suggested a rigorous schedule of PT to grow more muscle as soon as possible, This was a mad last hour attempt in the 3 months before we took off. I'm happy to say it worked.

In Sandpoint, I headed straight for our massage team to get their advice. Marianne was very helpful (sadly I think she passed away shortly after our trip) and told me about leg maintenance which I had never heard of. Every day after my ride she had me elevate my legs, put ice on my knees and massage the lactic acid out. New concept for me - I started adding that to my routine but couldn't heal over night.

There were three more days of riding before a day off. The next two were painful but not unbearable so I was optimistic. I had my spunk back but, looking back what I really needed was a couple of days off to repair properly. Of course that wasn't going to happen with our schedule.

(Ellen Lowe # 42) How easy it is to loose track of the "outside" world. Little, if any, news, radio, TV, newspapers. No time clocks, no dinners to cook or dishes to wash, no children to bath, no homework to help with, no nightmare morning commute. No driving or riding in a car. Upon meeting Ingrid Lynch from Washington State, I asked her what she did for a living. Her response was that during our Trek it didn't matter, we were all there for one purpose and one goal only. To cycle from Seattle to Atlantic City promoting the programs of the American Lung Association, anything and everything else was inconsequential. She never did tell me what she did, to this day I'm not sure I know.

(Marianne Brems #49) I've been getting pains in my feet. That's the only place. I'm hoping the Look pedals will help, along with my orthodontics. I enjoy this little resort town and a room and a bed. There's a lake but it's probably 55 degrees. I felt too lazy to commit to a swim in water that cold.

Chapter 3

Day 6 Sandpoint Idaho to Thompson Falls Montana 89 miles as remembered by Trekkers Guy Smith #280, Mary Fleming #27, Jana Chapman #41, Nancy Eiselt #6, Montana Highway Patrol Officer Harold Sanik, Ellen Lowe #42, Marianne Brems #49 and Jane Garrett #74

NOTE: Montana admitted to statehood November 8, 1889 is nicknamed the "Treasure State". It covers 147,046 square miles and would take us 10 days to cross.

(BIO JANE GARRETT #74) In 1989 I was beginning to bike a little more seriously, and take in some longer rides. I had experienced doing a couple of rides across different states, and some leisure rides on area bike paths. All in all though, I was pretty naïve as to what the extent of this ride would be.

I was working as a Registered Occupational Therapist in the school system; with children 3-21 years of age and multiple diagnoses. Therefore, I knew this would be a feasible thing to do- as I would have the time off.

A friend of mine had shown me the article regarding the ride in the American Lung Association Newsletter. I got excited about it immediately, then I thought about it more realistically for a bit, asked for the time off from work, and the rest is history. But yet I really didn't have any idea what the ride would entail. I just knew I was going to do it.

It seemed as though I was training every minute I had. But, how do you train for mountain passes in Iowa?Living in Davenport, along the Mississippi River. We have a fair share of steep hills in town. When I wasn't riding long distances, I would ride up and down the hills. They weren't all that easy. Some nights I would come home from riding them, almost in tears. How am I ever going to do this? But, once I have made a commitment, I don't turn back. My perseverance really did pay off.

(Jane Garrett #74) Today was one of my longest and hardest days. My body was revolting from riding, my muscles and rear end were just screaming.There was a group of about 3 or 4 of us who rode most of the way together. Singing songs along the way took away some of the pain, but no matter how you looked at it, it was TOUGH! I remember riding into the overnight town late in the day. There was a little grocery store right on our way to the headquarters for our overnight. We needed a few energy snacks to carry along in our bike bags. So we stopped and made a few purchases. I remember using our helmets as shopping baskets. Well, on to camp for the night. It was a mail stop also. What should we do first? It was getting dark and we needed to set up our tents, our meal time was also coming to a close. It went something like this…. We hurried to eat, hurried to set up our tents in the near darkness, hurried to get our showers in, hurried to see if we had any mail and then we called it a night never enough time.

The Iowa American Lung Association always came through with a wonderful gift in the mail at each of our mail stops. It was always fun to wonder what it would be; and who had been thinking of us with a box of goodies, a card or a letter. I'm sure our supporters never realized what our lives were like for the 47 days of Trek.

(Nancy Eiselt #6) I'm growing fond of this Trekker community already. I love the open road, the sound of bike wheels spinning down the pavement and of gears shifting, the feel of the wind on my face.... I've become attached to my little bike, the tent village, our gear truck, the shower truck and the blue port-a-potties...

BIO JANA CHAPMAN #41

In 1989 I was working for Boeing in Seattle, Washington. The people that I worked with put up a US map and followed my trip.

(Jana Chapman #41) My husband, Derek, (He was my boyfriend then) drove from Seattle to Thompson Falls on one day just to spend one night with me and he drove back to Seattle the next day. My twin daughters, Angela and Stefanie, who were graduating from high school the next week came with him. I was so excited to see my family I even beat the "Pace Line Group" into camp. I think the only one in camp before me was Warren. I was flying that day (emotionally and bike speed wise.) My daughters were very excited for me to do the Trek. They were fine with me not being able to attend their graduation ceremony. I was the last one to leave camp the next morning. I was crying so hard as I biked away I could barely see the road. I finally rode up to Skip from Florida and had to stop crying. He was having quite an adjustment to the weather, he was so cold he was just shaking. He made me laugh.

(Guy Smith #280) Today was one of the prettiest of the trip, along the banks of Lake Pend Oreille to Clark Fork and then all along the Clark River. I rode with Bonnie from Minneapolis and Marianne from Los Angeles mostly in a pace line, a method where

Sunrise 47

cyclists ride close together drafting each other to minimize energy expanded. We averaged 22 mph, not bad for hilly terrain. Everybody had to stop at the Monarch market in Lightning Creek to say "Happy Birthday" to Darrell, a highlight of our day and probably of his lifetime. In the afternoon I enjoyed the scenery with Michelle who I met at the checkpoint at Bull River station. We became the photo opportunity of the day" when we stopped for a nap at a hillside cemetery. The last ten miles were killers as we battled rough roads and strong, gusty head winds. But we had reached another milestone crossing into Montana, a state we would call home for the next 10 days. As we arrived at the Thompson Falls High School, I heard someone call my name from a car. Surprise! Pete had flown up from Denver in his "Piper Seneca" and had brought along Sue, Barron, Bernie, Cathleen and Curt. They spent the evening with us, shared stories with new friends, and lived the Trekker lifestyle for a day. They could tell I was very happy and had no need to be rescued. They pitched their tents alongside mine and we had a wonderful family reunion.

(**Harold Savik Montana Highway Patrol Officer**) Officer Savik who covers the route between Thompson Falls and Kalispell, said" the Transamerica Trekkers this year are the best he's ever seen in any event. Good Job"!

(**Mary Fleming #27**) I left Sandpoint at about 7 a.m., after breakfast which was served by the Boy Scouts and Brownies. The route took us around the northeast side of the Pend Orielle lake over gently rolling terrain. I saw my first unpleasant driver today. He was driving a beat up old pickup and as he passed a small group of riders in front of me he had his upper body outside of the truck yelling at the riders "get the hell off the road, assholes". This was a little shocking after the really friendly welcome that we had gotten from everyone. It was a good reminder though that there is a redneck segment no matter where you are and that it pays to be careful.

(**Ellen Lowe #42**) I remember Sue Proudfoot #79 with help from Nicki Tarant #97 going door to door in Thompson Falls in an all out effort to gather the last of her $5,000 in pledges, promising to shave her hair into a Mohawk if she reached her goal by nightfall. Come morning, Sue was wearing a huge smile and a new hairstyle, which proved to be the source of a very unique sunburn over the next few days.

(**Marianne Brems #49**) Mail is an uplifting thing. It seems strange that a little piece of paper from so far away can reach you and bring news.

This is real redneck country. I saw a pin which said "have gun will shoot". And a man at the service station was telling us that when he honked at three bikers riding three abreast, one of them flipped him off and the man said he had to have a talk with him. Now the biker has a loose tooth.

Day 7 Thompson Falls Montana to Elmo Montana 73 miles as remembered by Trekkers Guy Smith #280, Robert Sheldon #265, Mary Fleming #27, Nancy Eiselt #6, Ellen Lowe #42 and Marianne Brems #49

(Guy Smith #280) Today was cool, in the 40's. I had breakfast with my family at a restaurant before they took off for Yellowstone National Park. Because of the late start I rode mostly by myself, through beautiful mountains with almost no population centers; a few ranches and a lot of livestock were the major attractions. A large crowd gathered at the Long Branch Bar to listen to the NBA final game on the radio.Those who stayed to long regretted it, head winds and a very harsh, jolting road. I rode that stretch with Michelle, and we wondered why we were together every time the going got rough. Michelle had knee problems before the Trek and she rode with a very determined fast cadence, good for the knees. She was an inspiration to me because I tend to push to hard in a lower gear rather than use a fast cadence. The rode plunged sharply to Flathead Lake and our destination, the campground at Elmo State recreation area. I found a prime piece of real estate, a flat area right on the lake front, to pitch my tent. There

I met Tia and Mike, a couple who had met through the Trek and who already were deeply in love. They were talking marriage by the time we arrived in Atlantic City. Supper at Elmo was served by the Flathead Indians and featured breads we had never tasted.

(Robert Sheldon #265) "It was more than two feet long", reports Robert Sheldon when describing a mosquito that attacked him outside Elmo. With a wide smile on his face, Robert brought a 15 inch feather into the Blue Bus (this was our business office on wheels) as a trophy of his successful fight. He said, "On his final pass, I grabbed the beak and drove him into my spokes. Nearly knocked me off my bike."

(Mary Fleming #27) I slept really well last night and didn't wake up until the alarm went off at 5:30 a.m.For some reason I was feeling disoriented and couldn't quite get organized. The valley where we camped, was clouded in and it was quite damp and chilly. I decided to go to breakfast to allow my tights to dry out and to see what the weather was going to do.

By the time I got back it was still cold and damp so I decided to wear maximum clothing except for a warm jacket. I also brought a damp towel and clothing with the idea that I could lay it out to dry at one of the stops

I started out very slowly, which seemed reasonable and prudent on a full stomach. As I continued I realized that my energy level was not increasing at all which it generally does after about 5 miles. I stopped for a brief rest at 10 miles and again at 15. My hand was hurting badly in spite of the padding and everything was a major effort. It was a strange sensation because aside from my hand, I didn't hurt too much but I was practically in tears at times and wondered why I was doing this trip in the first place and considering whether or not there was any "honorable" way of getting out of it. What if I broke my arm or some other such thing? Would that give me a legitimate excuse to withdraw?

I never did find a good answer to my question but when I got to Plains at 24 miles and just before a five mile climb, I arranged for a ride into camp. I felt some sense of guilt for making use of the sag wagon, but the fact remains that my hand hurts and it's very difficult to ride with one hand.

The first thing I did in camp was pitch my tent and hang out wet clothes to dry. I lay down and went to sleep for 2 or 3 hours. When I woke up I felt better but still tired. I talked to the bike mechanic, Craig, he lowered my seat some and suggested that I might want to order a longer stem. It would take a couple of days. I will let him know tomorrow morning after I ride for awhile if I think we should do that.

We are camping at the Elmo State Recreation Area on the Flathead Lake. This is our first chance to experience what they mean when they call Montana "Big Sky Country". Dinner was provided on site. No cooking facilities, by the Lutheran Church Camp. Pasta Primavera, Salad, vegetables, several types of homemade bread, desserts of cakes and brownies. Very good and a real challenge for them under these conditions.

(Marianne Brems #49) Excellent Pasta Prima Vera and good conversation sitting out on the porch.

(Nancy Eiselt #6) I started out riding alone and stopped several times for photo's. After a bit of sun, we rode into a area of fog. It looked so beautiful - the heavy sky draped over the shoulders of the mountains created an air of real calm. At one point a big lump formed in my throat, as I thought about the beauty surrounding me and how lucky I am to live in this rich country.

(Ellen Lowe #42) I remember coming out of Thompson Falls towards Elmo, I was feeling unusually slow and listless in the 80+ degree heat and humidity. By the time I reached camp I had a major case of chills and fever. Shelley found me huddled inside my sleeping bag wearing a full sweat suit, so sick I could hardly move. After a night of endless vomiting and diarrhea, the EMT staff took me to a hospital in Kalispell, where I was diagnosed with a simple case of dehydration." A couple of hours hooked to an IV and I'd be fine" they said "Id be riding circles around the front runners" yeah right???? While others spent their "rest" day white water rafting, I was in a motel room attempting to gather my strength while chugging Gator Aid.

Day 8 Elmo Montana to West Glacier Montana 67 miles as remembered by Trekkers Mike Mitchell #1, Guy Smith #280, Mary Fleming #27, Sandy Kielmeyer Fredric #202, Karin Allen #29, and Marianne Brems #49

(Guy Smith #280) Today I rode again with Karin. I marveled at her constantly positive attitude even when we traversed 8 miles of gravel road torn up by construction; she truly enjoyed watching all the heavy equipment at work. We were happy to be back on paved road and enjoyed the fabulous view of Flathead Lake. Stopping for breakfast at a café we met Chuck and Susie, a Trekker couple from Seattle, who earn their living selling coffee from a gourmet stand. They knew good coffee! While we ate, two ambulances screeched down the road, and we worried about our friends who could be in trouble. The ambulances were not for Trekkers; but Karin and I had such powerful feelings that morning; perhaps a foreshadowing of things to come. Kalispell, Montana was a big city that excited me; I even thought it might be a good place to call home in the future. We ate our lunch on a wooden swing outside a local grocery store before tackling the long climb to Hungry Horse, home of the famous "House of Mystery".

Montana

Sunrise 47

The vortex phenomena were strange and convincing; we could stand almost sideways. There I realized how much fun we could have at a tourist trap when shared with fellow Trekkers The family atmosphere was truly beautiful. When we arrived at the campground in West Glacier, 612 miles were behind us. Perhaps for the first time I began to realize that we were truly going to cross the U.S. We partied late that night because the next day was a rest day, our first after 8 days on the road.

(Marianne Brems #49) With the wide open spaces and the Rockies looming majestically in the background, it feels so liberating in the same way that being at home feels constricting. I don't so much feel physically tired and in need of a rest day, but I feel that mentally it will be a relief.

(Mary Fleming #27) It's getting more and more difficult to get moving by 5:30a.m. I didn't get out of camp until 7-ish. Breakfast was at the Indian Cultural Center. I'm not sure if we are still on an Indian reservation or not. When I came back to the campground to get my gear loaded, I noticed a single lone phone booth at the entrance, that I had not seen before. I discovered later that the phone company had installed it just for our benefit for two days only.

It is the 8th day of riding, we were headed for West Glacier MT and a day off. Yea! I was sure that was all my knees needed. But as the day got long I was pushing to keep pace with the group that I had found to be in my speed category. I actually rode with these fine, compatible 5-7 people most of the rest of the Trek. We left at dawn most days, after one of them knocked on my tent to kindly wake me up and we usually made it to camp in the first 50. By arriving in the early afternoon we had time to relax a bit and get ready for the next day.

(Karin Allen #29) As we rode into Kalispell, we made one of my favorite "kitschy" stops of the whole trip to the "House of Mystery", one of those odd places where you find yourself standing at an angle. What a hoot!

(Mike Mitchell#1) My favorite meal so far.Barbecued steaks as big as a roast, or a half chicken, corn on the cob, baked beans and watermelon. I went with the steak and when I was finished I had to sit for a half hour before I could move. I'm keeping my eyes open for those big mosquitoes. They say some are as big as a small rat.

Day 9 Rest Day in West Glacier Montana 0 miles as remembered by Trekkers Guy Smith #280, Hugh Harold #334, Mary Fleming #27, Karin Allen #29, Ellen Lowe #42 and Marianne Brems #49

(**Guy Smith #280**) West Glacier is the west portal of the Rocky Mountains, and all during our rest day the snow-capped monsters peeked at us through nearby green foothills. We had a campfire show, and talent began to emerge - singers, guitarists and jokesters. A man named Jeff Green from Dallas announced that there would be a meeting of all "Jeff's" underneath the giant mosquito statue in the center of the campground. Thus "Team Jeff" was created, the first of many teams to be established in the weeks ahead. During our day off I experienced my first white water rafting on the Middle Fork of the Flathead river. Our guide "John" introduced us to some of the deeper holes in the river - "bone crusher", "Jaws" and "CBT" (Could be tense). The water was still bitterly cold, rushing down from melting snow just a few miles away. So I was slightly apprehensive when John suggested we stow our cameras in a waterproof box he provided. Our eyes opened wide as a wall of water rolled over us at the first rapids, the cold water evoking howls and squeals from men and women alike. Our raft was ambushed; as we passed under a bridge, other Trekkers dumped pails of water on us. It didn't matter as we were already soaked. Even John was worried when we got too close to a log which threatened to wipe us out, but we arrived safely with a great new experience to relate. I spent the rest of the day relaxing, writing postcards, chatting, napping and cleaning the Kid Krusader.

BIO HUGH HAROLD TREKKER #334

I was recently told by Kevin Collins that Hugh had suffered a stroke and is unable to communicate. Since he was a big part of this Trek I didn't want to exclude him. Shelley Lowe furnished me with an article that Hugh wrote and I am including portions of it in the book to honor Hugh.

(Hugh Harold #334) This was our first day off, in West Glacier National park. And what does an 87 mile per day Transamerica biker do on an "off day"? Would you believe white water rafting, in 17 foot,6 passenger rubber rafts.

Not everyone went. Some opted for horseback riding where one girl was thrown, broke her arm in three places, spent a week in the hospital, caught up to the Trek and stayed in one of the vans into Atlantic City. Also, a group of bikers, went mountain climbing, looking for the pure white mountain goats for which the Glacier Mountains are well known.

(Marianne Brems #49) People had that Saturday feeling today. Dawn, two Bonnie's, Pat and Robin warmed my heart so wonderfully at breakfast this morning. We sat for an hour and talked about self-esteem and children and control. You just want to touch Pat's hair every time you see it.

(Mary Fleming #27) This is our first rest day. We are at a campground just outside the park. Breakfast was from 5 a.m. to 10 a.m. I woke up at 7:30.The latest since we started and I wasn't the only one. There was a lot of noisy partying going on until late last night.

If it wasn't for a large, noisy bird cawing over my tent, I expect that I would have slept a lot later.

Breakfast was a huge pancake with eggs and sausage. There are a number of activities available for today including white water rafting, horseback riding, park tours, trips into town etc.

I intend to hang around camp and read or maybe sleep. The energy level of some of these people is just incredible. I have always thought of myself as a high energy person, but to me, the idea of doing anything today that requires exertion is just unthinkable.

(Karin Allen #29) By the time we got to West Glacier for our first day off, I was feeling great! I found myself chuckling when I read a letter from my boyfriend saying how sorry he was that I was so miserable. Me? I was having a GREAT time! Besides the friends I had made before the Trek, Terri Sears and Nancy Eiselt, I had made a number of new friends since the Trek had started including Guy Smith, Tom Rowe, Jeff Green, Chuck and Suzy Beek, and many others. There really was a feeling of camaraderie and "can do" spirit that made me feel as though I could pedal on indefinitely.

(**Ellen Lowe #42**) I remember Guy Smith #280 being my guardian angel. He vowed to help make sure I was safe as we headed out of West Glacier. At even the slightest slow down on my part, Guy would shout, "I have to stop to water a tree".Never before or since have either of us watered so many trees!

Day 10 West Glacier Montana to St Mary Montana 52 miles as remembered by Trekkers Guy Smith #280, Mary Fleming #27, Michael McKendry #219,George Gee #228, Roger Whidden #190, Hubert "Woody" Wood #237, Nancy Ackles #124, Mike Mitchell #1 and Ellen Lowe #42

BIO HUBERT "WOODY" WOOD #237

In 1989 I was employed as a probation/parole officer in Lancaster Co PA. I had major surgery the summer of 1988 and was looking for a challenge. I decided to ride on the Trek just six weeks before the ride began after talking to a neighbor who worked for the American Lung Association.

(**Hubert "Woody" Wood #237**) Woody says "The best day of the Trek is very difficult to choose. If pushed, I would choose riding the "Going to the Sun" through Glacier National park. If heaven exists, it must look something like that."

BIO GEORGE GEE #228

In 1988 I read an article in our employee's paper, an engineer was retiring at 60 and planning on a bicycle trip across the United States from Sacramento CA to Washington DC. In October I read in the San Francisco Chronicle of a meeting on a Transamerica Bicycle Trek Ride for 1989. I went to the meeting and was very ex-

Sunrise 47

cited about the trip. I bought a new 18 speed bicycle. I hadn't been on a bike for 20 years. I had accumulated 10 weeks of vacation time and decided to use these days instead of retiring to go on this trip. I postponed my retirement after I completed the Trek seven months later.

(George Gee #228) I was surprised there was so much snow at the summit of Logan pass. After touring the visitor center I headed down to St Mary's. I had to make many stops. I tried to warm up. The wind chill was so cold, my fingers felt like they were in ice water.

(Guy Smith #280) Wednesday morning was cloudy with a high overcast and drizzle. We were advised to carry warm clothes, for this was our day to cross the Rocky Mountains. Our route was the famous "Going to the sun" highway across Glacier National Park. I had arranged to ride with Ellen from Los Angeles who had been ill from dehydration and had even spent a night in the hospital. Her daughter Shelley, also a Trekker started with us until she was assured that her Mom was strong enough for the strenuous climb ahead. The road was pleasantly flat following the banks of lake McDonald, and the scenery became more spectacular with each turn in the road as we neared the lofty peaks. Waterfalls were every where and the deer seemed to be congregating along our route to cheer us on. After we crossed Logan Creek the road grade began a steep ascent. From there it was 11 vertical miles to the top of Logan pass. Each switchback of the road revealed breathtaking scenery and we stopped often to enjoy and photograph it. The peaks on either side of us loomed up to 11,000 feet, but the highway sneaks through at Logan Pass (6,646 feet**)**.

All day the clouds got lower and darker at the top it was cold and rainy;huge snowdrifts lined both sides of the road which had just been plowed open two days before. But nothing could dampen our exuberance at reaching this climatic point. We warmed up at the fireplace in the Logan Pass Visitor's Center at the summit before braving the elements for the descent. The down grade was steep and tempting, but we didn't dare go too fast on the wet roads. It warmed up quickly on the way down especially after we stopped for hot chicken soup. Summer was back. Home for the evening was Johnson's camp ground, we pitched our tents among small aspen trees at the eastern slope of the Rockies in St Mary Montana.

(Mary Fleming #27) Beautiful day today I left camp at about 6:30 a.m. after picking up a pre-ordered bag lunch across the road and a bottle of Gatorade at the little market that was open just for us. We then headed for the "Going to the sun" highway which crosses the continental divide at Logan Pass.

For the first twenty miles we rode along Lake McDonald. After that we began an 11 mile climb that took us up 3,700 feet to Logan Pass. The pass had only been opened the week before and there was still at least six feet of snow at the top. Starting next Thursday, they will have a regulation that requires any bicycles to be off the pass by 11a.m. I didn't get to the top until 11:30. They say the grade is about 6% which is not too bad. Eleven miles is a bit long, but the views were beautiful. It was cloudy and a little drizzly. At the top it was 46 degrees, according to my thermometer.

I changed my damp shirts at the top for dry ones, put on a warm jacket and gloves for a fast run down. I ate my sack lunch there, but was still hungry, so I stopped at the Rising Sun recreation area for another lunch.

The wild flowers are great and varied. I can only identify a couple (Indian Pint Brush and Forget Me Notes) but there are many more. The road was very narrow and wet but most of the automobile drivers were very patient and considerate.Many of them waving at us when they went by.

I think I'm going to miss the mountains, trees and lakes of the country we have been traveling thorough. Tomorrow we climb up onto a plateau and begin the plains portion of the trip. Even now we have left the evergreens pretty much behind and are in the area of birch trees and grassland

BIO MIKE MCKENDRY #219

I had decided at 16 that crossing the country was something I wanted to do. I had an AM radio station on a late night program while doing homework my freshman year of college at the University of Massachusetts when I heard a phone interview with some 1988 Trekkers. They gave the contact information for how to join and I started my training in January of 1989. In 1989 I was 19 years old and I had gone back to school to finish a bachelor's degree in music education.

(Michael McKendry #219) I left the group for five days starting with the morning we left St. Mary's in Montana. We were 18 miles from the Canadian border. I was just planning on going and coming back to say I was there. I asked a few Trekkers if they might be interested in going with me but none were. The morning out of St Mary's there was a 30mph tailwind on the way to the border and the road was flat. It was amazing riding at 30 with no wind noise just the whir of the tires beneath me. I was able to get up to 48 on the flat.Could have easily gone faster if my gearing had permitted it. Some interesting things happened over the next five days including staying with an elderly woman with the same last name as mine. The road I planned to take back to the Trek on route 2 turned out to be gravel. That day with the tailwind I logged 140 miles. Another day was 130 miles from Medicine Hat, Alberta to

Havre, Montana. I took a few breaks that day, including a short lift from a park ranger. But I left Medicine Hat at 8:00 a.m. and arrived in Havre at around 11 p.m. a long day.

You probably remember the day with the 30 mph headwinds. I was by myself, and it was breaking my spirit. The 15 hour day before probably had something to do with it. So I hitched a ride in an empty freight train for about 40 miles. At one of the Indian reservations (Fort Peck) a huge wind and dust storm came up. This was the night everybody stayed overnight in Poplar. A toothless guy and his wife from Poplar were there at the store and insisted they drive me there. They also made me supper and invited me to stay with them for the night. I tended to be pretty lucky with people taking me in like that. I didn't feel guilty about the rides I took, because all in all, I probably did about as many miles all told as everybody else. And it was real important to catch up again. I rejoined the group the next morning as we left Poplar.

BIO ROGER WHIDDEN #190 The 1989 Bike Trek was before children! Recognizing that it could be the last hurrah at least for several year's. I was able to negotiate seven weeks off from my teaching - Karate and Tai Chi to children and adults. I also had good timing relative to a small window between building houses as well. My bike training until that time was mostly commuting approx. 100 miles a week, 6 months a year. Though I was in top shape through Martial Arts and athletics, I did bike through the winter prior to Trek. The mental toughness and 'butt time" was absolutely necessary to do all the miles vertically and enjoyably. I wanted to see the country and help support a good cause(The American Lung Association).

(Roger Whidden #190) I'm at dinner with Audrey (very fast athlete, attractive women in her mid 20's) at St. Mary's after climbing and descending Rockies (I passed a car at 65 mph). She is telling me of this guy Steve who keeps falling off his bike. I sense Steve and I are going to have a lot of personal time together. Steve and I arrange to ride a tandem. I want to give him the ride of his life.

(Nancy Ackles #124) Going up Glacier pass where the cars were moving only slightly faster than the bikes and taking in the scenery, a line of riders relayed the message up the line, "Car Back" (warns the riders ahead that a car is coming) At the head of the line, the front seat passenger rolled down the window and said, "Mr. Carbek, your friends are calling to you".

(Mike Mitchell #1) I mentioned in the acknowledgements that I saw Dave Shaw lose his temper a couple of times(justifiably so) This was one of those days. We were in camp waiting for the food line to open. It was a difficult location and the ladies serving had done a terrific job. As the volunteers started serving one of the Trekkers (I won't use his name) started yelling at the ladies that the food was horrible and how was he going to eat this crap. He became so abusive that one of the ladies started crying. The next thing we saw was Dave taking the Trekker by the arm and taking him out into the woods. We couldn't hear what was said but we could see the flames and smoke coming out of Dave's mouth. A few minutes later the Trekker returned apologized to the ladies and skipped dinner. Way to go Dave.

(Ellen Lowe #42) I remember the cold, rain and sleet as we climbed 6646 feet to Logan pass and the Continental Divide. In the lodge at the top I tried to dry my tights with the blower style hand dryers in the ladies room and melted the sleeve of my tyvek Trek jacket in front of the fireplace. Barely warm, I headed down the mountain with sleet stinging my cheeks and pounding loudly on my helmet. Welcome to the big, blue sky country of Montana.

Day 11 St Mary Montana to Shelby Montana 89 miles as remembered by Trekkers Mary Fleming #27, Hugh Harold #334, Guy Smith #280, Cynthia Roberts #38, Ellen Lowe #42 and Marianne Brems #49

(Mary Fleming #27) Much of the travel today was through the Blackfoot Indian Reservation. The villages are rather bleak, with no trees or vegetation planted near the homes. One home, out by itself has a 10 foot wall built on the windward side of the house. A row of trees would have created a windbreak and looked a lot better. It would be interesting to know more about Indian culture and sociology.

(Guy Smith #280) Today was a real revelation to many Trekkers. The day began with a steep six mile climb to the great plain. From there the road stretched out for miles - no trees, nothing but the grasslands and the heavens, truly "Big Sky" country. We had entered the Blackfeet Indian Reservation and the tall grasses were bending to the East in the strong wind. Not everybody realized it at once, but as Trekkers learned the meaning of "tail wind" exhilaration filled their faces. We could cruise at 16 mph while barely pedaling. With only normal effort we could go 25 mph on a level road. Scott, our tri-athlete from Iowa, was clocked at 37 mph by one of the support vehicles. The best part was that we could keep this pace up all day. We breezed through Cut Bank, MT where a huge penguin statue held a sign claiming Cut Bank to be the coldest town in the USA. It was very hot on that day, but nobody cared; every conversation was about the wind. We enjoyed fabulous home made apple pie at a restaurant there, the owner had reportedly baked all week in preparation of our arrival. But not everything was going so wonderfully; this day began my rash of flat tires.

They were all alike a slow leak that always occurred when I was having the most fun. I finally solved the problem six days later when I removed "Mr Tuffy" a liner I had put inside the tire that was rubbing against the tube at high speeds and causing the leaks.

(Hugh Harold #334) We had a young lady biker with us from Russia who rode with us on invitation as our special guest. However, she was delayed in London for 10 days with Visa problems and rode with us starting in Montana instead of Seattle. Her name is Rusiko Roakidze. We became good friends. Since we had a problem with each others name, we jokingly called each other by our bike number. I was called "334", she was "301". She thought I was ancient history when told that the #334 was used in recognition of my World War II submarine number. I guess Ron Stewart (#262), my graduate student buddy, looked on me as being ancient also. His dad served on the 334 with me."

BIO CYNTHIA ROBERTS #38

I chose to do the 1989 Trek since I had just retired. RIF-US Army -Benet Labs, technical librarian for SMCAR-CCB. Most of the scientists supported me by a $35.00 pledge. They were sick of war and I guess listening to me talk about going on the Trek and my training provided an ease to their burdens. I had ended 27 years of teaching to return home to care for aged parents who lived to be 87 (Pop) and 97 & 3 months (Mom).

(Cynthia Roberts #38) Today was really special because of a lovely family (the Anderson's) who did my laundry for me so I could see a historical museum in Shelby. The whole trip was great but I really appreciated the "Blue Bus Crew", our great mechanics, the parrot people who took care of our showers and toilets, the Cber's who kept us current on the weather and any problems on the road, and all of the groups that prepared our meals. I really enjoyed the young people and the sing a longs at night.

(Marianne Brems #49) The Rockies changed immediately to plains today after a short six mile climb. I was amazed to see the mountains on the right and essentially the Midwest on the left all at once.

We saw some very broken down towns. They were hardly towns. I suppose the Indians are forced to live there.

(Michael Scenery #219) I was riding with Eric one day when we came upon a Dan Henry (directions in the road that tell us which way to go) it had a squiggle coming out of the circle. The trip tik said "jog left, then right". Eric got off his bike and commenced to jog to the left, then to the right, got back on his bike and continued on.

(Ellen Lowe #42) I remember the humongous, hungry mosquitoes of Montana!! Shelley, first applied sun screen, then later applied mosquito repellant, caused a chemical interaction which turned her skin bright purple. Thank goodness it all rinsed off in the shower, no damage done.

Montana

Day 12 Shelby Montana to Havre Montana 107 miles as remembered by Trekkers Mary Fleming #27, Guy Smith #280, Gene Armone #63, Woody Wood #237 and Miranne Brems #49

NOTE: *Jim Fletter # 80 and Debbie Fletter # 194 were the only father-daughter team on the Trek.*

(**Mary Fleming #27**) We narrowly missed a big storm. We got a little rain, but the hail (the size of golf balls) and the heavy winds, hit south and east of us. Today we did our longest day and really lucked out on the weather. It was cloudy most of the day, the wind blowing strongly from the northwest and the terrain was relatively flat and level. I had my radio on a lot because there wasn't a lot of variety to the landscape. The Sweetwater mountain's were off to the north. In the first half of the day the Bear Paws were to the south as we approached Havre.

(**Woody Wood #237**) Woody said " I heard a story about Chuck Beek Trekker #43 going into a bar and spraying everyone with his water bottle including the locals that were there. Later as the group was heading back to camp a pickup truck began to follow them. As the truck slowly approached Chuck, a man with a bucket of water soaked him and drove away laughing."

(**Guy Smith #280**) Today's trip from Shelby to Havre was a long one, 107 miles, and I persuaded my riding companion, Ellen from Alaska to start early. She was struggling with a very bad cold; but we kept a great pace as the tail winds blew again all day and we cruised through the tiny towns like robotic toys. Crossing the Sweetgrass Hills, we had our last view of the Rockies to the West.Before us lay endless miles of Great Plains with each town being nothing more than a café or a food store. Our destination, Havre was a good sized city, the home of Northern Montana University where we camped on the lawn and ate in the college cafeteria.

BIO GENE ARMONE #63

I started the Transamerica on June 5, 1989 and finished it June 24, 2006. Everyone said I finished it in July 1989 but I always felt there was an asterisk next to that date. There were many more heroic stories to Transamerica 1989, and far more painful injuries, so my story is just one of a hundred others; all personal and equally fulfilling.

It all started in July, 1988, when the Transamerica finished in my hometown, Atlantic City. I clearly remember reading the Sunday paper about the finish and the entire event. It was in my mind all day and at dinner I said to my wife, Cindy, "I'm going to do that next year", without any further comment she said "OK" and never wavered in her support. The next day I made the same statement to my business partner, whose comment was instantly, "what do we need to do to make that happen?" Without that kind of support from those closest to me, there would have been no Trek for me.

The first 1000 miles were enjoyable, revealing, challenging and transitional from my past life and friends to new priorities and relationships. Physical adjustments were necessary, as no amount of training could have prepared you for the demands now being made on my body. Knowing no one on the Trek, everyone was a new acquaintance and a potential long term relationship. For me this was a slow, deliberate process, with lifelong implications.

(Gene Armone #63) Then came that fateful, life changing day, June 16, 1989. It was the 102nd mile of a 107 mile day into Havre, Montana, in the middle of nowhere. A slip in concentration, a double tractor trailer going 75 mph, speed bumps on the side of the road, all resulted in a tumble, then pain, all happening in slow motion. A fellow Trekker stopped to help, a blur in my memory. After riding the final 5 miles into camp, I was checked out by our EMT and told we were going to the ER.

It took only 30 seconds for the doctor to look at the x-rays to conclude a broken collar bone and a statement "that's all for you". "What happens if I keep going?" I asked. "If you fall, you could puncture a lung". "Then I won't fall" was my immediate reply. Fortunately for me the bone was broken, but not separated. As I have said hundreds of times the pain of going home would have been worse than any pain that I would endure riding, but that was not logic talking.

I went back to camp, had dinner and spent the worst emotional night of my life. My fellow Trekkers were sympathetic, supportive and extremely helpful, but I was alone in the middle of a crowd. I decided to hold off any decision until the next day and tried to sleep. The next morning the pain was there, but I focused on if I were to continue, how or if, it could be done? Craig, our mechanic, suggested changing my handlebars to mountain bike style, but the pain I was still experiencing was causing serious doubts as to my physical ability to continue.

I rode in the van the next day and quickly concluded that finishing the Trek that way was not an option.It was continue or go home. We played a softball game in Malta that night and not being able to play was very depressing. I had to be part of the Trek or out, nothing in-between. I decided to give it a try the next day and see what happens. Dave Shaw suggested that I ride in the van halfway to the B&B café and ride in from there. Finish on a high note rather than quit halfway. I still hadn't called my wife; I couldn't until I knew what I was going to do.

So here I was at the B&B Café and ready to try. All of a sudden a guardian angel appeared in the name of Tim Williams #147. I knew him from the group but never rode with him. He asked if I minded if he rode along and he ended up staying with me for the next week, watching my back, handing me water, and just talking and providing emotional support. Other Trekkers were supportive, both in riding and in camp helping with my tent and food tray. After a few days I knew I could do it and called home, telling my wife what happened and my decision to continue.

The rest of my Trek was no more notable from that of fellow bikers. I developed a regular riding group, "Studs and Babes," and shared the common experiences of the group.

When we arrived in Atlantic City I had already decided to just say goodbye and ride off without further contact. The person I am outside the Trek is not the same person I was on the Trek, and that was the person I wanted them to remember. And that is what I have done over the years with no regrets.

Whenever I have told the story of my Trek, I always felt obligated to talk about the 150 miles I missed in the van and saying I planned to go back someday and finish the Trek. Well, now in 2006, I have finally done that. As part of a road trip this summer, with my wife serving as support again, I completed those miles on June 23 and 24, 2006.

At age 59 and with minimal training, 90 miles followed by 60 miles was a challenge to say the least. The memories and feelings quickly returned, especially when a train blew it's whistle at me in the middle of nowhere. But in spite of that, it was not the same. It became obvious that my fellow Trekkers were the Transamerica memories and experiences rather than the ride itself. Things were the same, but different, the B&B Café was no longer there, there were more hills than I remembered, but the scenery was just as stunning. There was nothing left in my tank physically and emotionally, when I finished, but that chapter in my life is now complete and continues to be a major part of who I am.

Day 13 Havre Montana to Malta Montana 91 miles as remembered by Trekkers Guy Smith #280, Mary Fleming #27, Sandy Kielmeyer Fredric #202, Mike Mitchell #1, Marianne Brems #49 and Kevin Collins #25

(**Guy Smith #280**) On Saturday I was a Sweep. 'Sweeper's" are volunteer cyclists who leave camp last and try to stay behind the entire Trek all day, keeping track of slow movers and people who might have problems. When the sweeper's pass, the road support vehicles move ahead. We had six vans that patrolled the route, manned by volunteer staff who provided water, minor repairs, emergency medical treatment, transportation for the weary, radio communications and plenty of encouragement. Sweeper's work best in pairs; I rode with Wendy, my friend from Boulder Colorado. We surely picked an easy day with tail winds and nothing much to see except tiny towns on the Fort Belknap Indian Reservation. Sweepers usually have a very long day, arriving in camp near dusk around 9:30 or later. But Wendy and I signed in at 5:15 p.m., reportedly the earliest sweep ever. For a small town, Malta had a lot to offer us. It got my vote for the best meal so far on the trek, shrimp, crab, and macaroni and cheese. We played a softball game against the local team, the Trekker cheering squad was 300 strong, everybody who wasn't on the playing field. We lost the game but won in the stands where kegs of beer bolstered spirits and sweetened the bait for the mosquitoes who were the real winners of the evening.The party continued at a bar were we celebrated two birthdays. With Trekkers dancing wildly to live rock and roll, the locals couldn't believe that we had biked 91 miles that day I went to bed late but planned to start early, hoping to find a church along the way.

(**Kevin Collins #25**) As I was riding alone (and making good time) I spotted a small object in midair coming at me. By the time I realized it was a bee I had no time to get my mouth closed completely. He hit my mouth and lodged in it until I was able to rip him away. Needless to say he did get his stinger in and for the next three hours it felt like the dentist had just given me Novocain. No trouble with mosquito's, just a bee.

(**Mary Fleming #27**) It was a little warmer today with the sun shining. The wind was from the Southwest at about 15 mph, I would guess. The cool wind kept the temperatures from getting to high. Some of the local Havre kids decided to hassle us last night and were setting off firecrackers and yelling " Time to get up" in the middle of the night. I guess they thought it was funny. Other people in town were very friendly. On the way out I was asked about the trip by 3 or 4 people and wished well.

The countryside, east of Havre, is hilly with lot's of trees and small farms. The area has gas, oil, ranching and farming as it's primary activities. As you proceed east the land becomes more level as the route follows the Milk river. Eventually, it is mostly large acreage crop land with the only indication of the river being a line of trees weaving back and forth in the distance.

It was a long ride and I took several good long breaks and numerous photo stops. I was bouncing around from being tired and dragging to having lots of energy and just zipping along. By just keeping my cadence high (80-90) and with the help of the wind I was flying up a long gentle hill at 25 mph, sweeping past other riders. I'm still not sure if the others were just going slowly or what, but it was a strange sensation.A very powerful feeling with the bike and me working as a unit. I feel tired but not exhausted. I am counting the days until our next rest day though. Three more to go (93, 69 and 79)Doesn't sound to bad. Two more Montana stops and then it's into North Dakota.

(Nancy Ackles #124) Nancy shares one of her good memories "I was shopping in a strip mall in Montana with Dottie Potts, (I think it was Dottie) we were looking for socks. A boy about ten years old came up to us and said "You guys have got guts". Middle aged women don't often get that kind of compliments from little boys.

(Sandy Kilmeyer Fredric #202) Today the pain got so bad that after we stopped for a Huckleberry ice cream cone and took pictures with a little man and bear in a car, I told my group to go on without me,that I needed a bit more rest. I hadn't told anyone how bad my knees were - everyone had their own stuff to deal with and this was my problem alone. I didn't want to bring anyone down, we always tried to lift each others mood, keep it light, humorous and give each other encouragement.

But after I rested again I knew I had to move before my muscles got cold and stiff. A nightmare ensued. Every turn of the pedal was very painful and my left knee would sort of "lock up". It would hardly bend. I went slower and slower as one Trekker after another passed me. I acted like I was fine, just sight seeing. The last few miles I mostly used my right leg to power the bike. A very odd system I figured out, I sort of kicked the pedal forward and down with my left foot and when it came to the top (I had taken it out of the clamp) I then made the rotation with my right leg.Back and forth at a snails pace, but it kept me on my bike and moving. Dusk ended as a sweep vehicle came by and said I needed to get to camp and did I need a ride. I was determined to ride every mile on my bike so I said I was fine and they said I was almost there. I was the last one into camp but I made it and by my own power.

I think the next day off saved me. By the grace of God and with my faithful attention to my new leg maintenance program I had almost no knee problems the rest of the journey. Whew!!

(Mike Mitchell #1) Close to another century day with 91 miles ahead of me. Picked up a tail wind shortly into the ride and knew it was going to be a fun day. The miles and the towns flew by, Lohman, Chinook, Zurich, Harlem, Fort Belknap and Dodson. The Bear Paw mountains remained off to the south. Before I knew it I was in Malta and had time to take a nice hot shower and enjoy the rest of the afternoon doing nothing. Went to the baseball game and tipped a few brews and got to bed early. Some of the group went to a party and were a little noisy getting back to camp but it only lasted a few minutes and after all the zippers closed everyone settled in for the night.

(Marianne Brems #49) There's something about country western music that suit's the cadence of bike riding. There really can be something quite euphoric about music, the bike and the wide open spaces.

Everything happens big and fast on the Trek or it doesn't happen at all. Gayle Delanty is an advanced woman. She's compassionate, she's a good listener and she has that reserve that let's you know she doesn't have to talk about herself to feel important.

Day 14 Malta Montana to Ft. Peck Montana 93 miles as remembered by Trekkers Guy Smith #280, Beth DeRooy #19, Mary Fleming #27, Ellen Lowe #42) and Marianne Brems #49

(Guy Smith #280) The Sunday ride from Malta to Fort Peck was a carbon copy of the last two days; warm with strong tail winds. We were truly being spoiled. I started off alone hoping to get to Saco in time for church, but it was to far. I met Michelle there and quickly we departed Saco, the mosquito capital of the world. At the Hinsdale café Trekkers were tempted by the "Double D Dare" eat all of the $12.95 breakfast in an hour and get it free. It was only 3 eggs, 1 lb of hash browns, 2 pieces of toast, 6 sausages and 3 pancakes. To Scott it was easy until the pancakes arrived. They were each almost an inch thick and so big that they flopped over the sides of the plate onto the table. Scott ran out of time with only three quarters of a pancake left. Several others tried, but all paid for their meal despite wild cheering from the Trekker fans. I bought "Millie" a small cheerleader doll who was to be my mascot for the rest of the Trek. She withstood a lot of abuse from Trekkers

Sunrise 47

and road grime along the way, but she was clean and new that day as we passed the 1000 mile mark on the journey. Like all milestones, we memorialized the moment with lots of photo's at the spot where"1,000"was painted on the roadway. I had my first Blizzard at the Dairy Queen in Glasgow, it is a very thick milk shake with cookies, nuts or candies blended into it. As the Trek wore on, at a Milwaukee Dairy Queen, "Team Blizzard" would be born. At the end of the day we needed the energy because the tail winds died and the hills became plentiful from Glasgow to the Fort Peck Indian Reservation. Dinner that evening was in an old hotel, and some of us went to se "I Do, I Do" a play with one actor and one actress.

BIO BETH DEROOY TREKKER #19.

I left my daughter, 9 years old in 1989 at home with her dad and grandparents. It was a big deal to leave her for 47 days. But I had to do it because cycling across the country was an often verbalized dream. When I was 11, my parents took me and my siblings to Holland, the land of their births. It was there that I observed people commuting via bicycle ,and traveling with panniers. I was smitten. I cycled on the dykes and town and country streets nearby the homes of relatives, and dreamed of someday, as a young adult, cycling through Europe, or exploring the world anywhere on the seat of a bike. In my mid twenties I did some long distance cycling, fully loaded for a week at a time. In 1989 in my forties, I was oh-so-ready to scratch another on-the -road itch. I was mentally and emotionally primed to say, unequivocally," that's for me"!!! when I heard about Transamerica. Raising money for ALA was a piece of cake. I thought it would be tough, but the money flowed in effortlessly in response to my reaching out, informing people, getting them excited for me and for the cause.

(Beth Derooy #19) Beth a retired nurse remembers this day well. She said "The day that was life altering for me was the day cycling to Poplar. I somehow was not able to keep up with various folk I had been riding with earlier during the day and urged them to go ahead: I would plug along on my own. The ride seemed interminable. The miles seemingly went on forever. My legs wanted to come to a grinding halt with every pedal stroke. There was no other rider in sight. I expected camp in a half hour, and then in the next half hour. The half hours passed one after another after another. It was hot. I was crying. I was screaming with discomfort and frustration, gritting my teeth with angry determination begrudging my weary body. Finally, late in the day, I pulled into camp. My friend Elaine led me to my tent which she had set up for me, along with a cold beer. I burst into tears of gratitude. We sat on the grass, facing the gear truck, mellowing with each cold slurp. What I saw next made me break out in heart rendering sobs. Steve Andersen, a fellow rider who had a neurological disease that rendered him spastic, climbed up the stairs into the gear truck. He looked WAY more tired than I. He took each step slowly, hanging onto the rail, I thought how much tougher his day must have been than mine. And of how EVERY day; was much more challenging than my day could ever be with my wholly functional body. I had a good friend to share this with at the time.Thank you Elaine. And something changed deep in my bones. No matter how weary or worn out I might feel, I would see Steve, and know it could be worse. thank you Steve. You helped me grow up a little bit that day I will never forget you.

(Mary Fleming #27) Last night our group was challenged by the Malta Chamber of Commerce to a softball game. I didn't go, but I understand that we lost. I heard several people say that they would rather not play or that if they did, it would not be an all out effort, in order to be sure that they didn't injure themselves.

No announcements have been made, but we have had one person in the hospital briefly for dehydration, one person downed by railroad tracks, one hit by a car (no serious injury), one fall that resulted in a broken collar bone and a few cases of road rash. We have lots of people sitting around with ice on their knees at break times.

We had another 90 mile day. I did well and felt well for 42 miles, was tired but moved well to 56 miles, slowed down some to 70 and was very uncomfortable for the last 20 miles.

We continued to follow the valley of the Milk River, until Glasgow, where we cut across hills to Fort Peck Lake. The Fort Peck dam was built in the 30's to provide irrigation and power. The terrain was very open and relatively level, much the same as the last few days.

(Ellen Lowe #42) I remember Chuck and Susie Beek who own coffee stands in Washington State. They carried their own coffee beans and coffee grinder for fresh brewed coffee every day.

(Marianne Brems #49) I never knew that so many people snored, it seems to be mostly men. We are so visible to each other. You can't do anything that someone else won't see, except in your own tent. Even if you bring something or someone in people know. It's uncomfortable to be so close to everyone's bodily functions. I get tired of seeing people gong in and out of the bathroom doors and knowing exactly when they wash and shave. You even hang out your dirty laundry here for everyone to see. Even touching out here is extreme. I think those not involved sexually generally are not being touched at all. It's like you get all or none. And you can't really have a conversation when you're supposed to go single file and you're always watching for cars. I gave six people back rubs after dinner and all of them almost fell into their plates.

Day 15 Poplar MT to Williston ND 79 miles as remembered by Trekkers Guy Smith #280, Mary Fleming #27, Mike Mitchell #1, Nancy Eiselt #6, Marianne Brims #49 and Jane Garrett #74

NOTE: *We were often asked what type of bike do you have to have to ride on a long distance like the Trek? People have done the Trek on all types of bikes from light weight racers to mountain bikes. Recommended is a lightweight touring bike, which the manufacturers call a "sport bike".*

(Guy Smith #280) Today I got a very early start, hoping to beat the head winds. But Mother Nature spared us. With a high overcast the winds had become light and variable, swept through by the evening storms. I started the day with Karin, Nancy and Terri all from Seattle. The four of us later became "Team Blizzard". I was surely the envy of all the guys riding with these three beautiful ladies. Luck wasn't with me though, a flat tire separated me from them near Culbertson. It wasn't my day. When I got another flat just 5 miles farther down the road, I was rescued by Gail from Seattle who loaned me her spare tube. Something really was wrong. The tire went flat again in a few miles, just as I arrived at the "Welcome to North Dakota" sign. I was frustrated and angry. Fortunately Duane was in a support van there and he changed the tire and fixed a spoke that was probably causing the problem. Anyway, I had no more flats on the rear tire the rest of the Trek. My three flats in one day wasn't the record; Julie had five back in Washington, all caused by a bad spoke. Entering North Dakota was a major landmark it had taken us ten days to cross Montana the largest state on the Trek. Of course photo's marked the occasion. I connected with Karen again as we neared Williston, North Dakota. There was a surprise welcome for us with banners and cheers from a group of kids and moms called the "kids in the park". I stopped to get pictures taken with them.

(Jane Garrett #74) In the Midwest we have thunderstorms with lightning, thunder, wind and precipitation. Many people in other parts of the United states have the thunderstorms without the lightning and thunder. When we got in from riding today, we rushed to get our tents put up before a thunderstorm hit us. We had eaten and taken our showers, before the action started. Well, I got hunkered down in my tent, only after making sure my ground cloth was tucked in and all the stakes were tight. When the storm hit I was in my tent, waiting to see what kind of weather it was going to bring us. I could hear people and see people outside getting excited about the lightning and thunder that they were experiencing for the first time!! It was truly amazing what some of us take for granted,and what others have never experienced. Another incredible act of mother nature.

(Mary Fleming#27) The meals at Fort Peck were not the greatest, not very satisfying. The local little theatre had a play called "I Do, I Do" which I went to see. It had two characters, a husband and wife from the day of their marriage, to 50 years later, when they moved out of their house into an apartment. The message, that a woman is only happy when she has a man to love, seemed a little bit out of date.

We started the ride with a little bit of a tailwind, but within an hour or two it was coming from the southeast at about a 45 degree angle with a fairly large force 20-30 mph. Most of us took advantage of every possible stopping point. By early afternoon, the temperature was up to 95 degrees. I was riding with Jim and trying to draft but I almost had to ride next to him to get any effect. It took a lot of experimentation to find the right spot and then I was restricted by the Montana law which says you can't ride two abreast and you can't ride to the left of the white line. Whenever I got tired and lost him I realized that the drafting was helping more than I thought.

The heat made me really miserable. I poured water on my head, on my neck bandana, on my shirt, all of which helped briefly, but with the high winds, everything dried very quickly. Whenever I refilled with cold water it would be warm water within a half hour. For some reason the warm water didn't seem to have the cooling effect on the body that you would expect with evaporation.

The last twelve miles included several miles of road construction. Where they had finished, the road surface was great. Part of it was still gravel and was difficult to ride on. In this 12 mile stretch I found it necessary to stop every 2 or 3 miles just to wet down, drink and rest my bottom and hands. When you are pushing constantly against a wind you hang on tighter and never get a chance to just coast and take some pressure off the sore spots. I was extremely tired when we arrived.

I showered set up my tent (carefully placing it in the limited shade area), went to dinner (which was probably the best we have had so far) and came back to an impending thunderstorm. I put on the rain fly and secured the tent stakes. The tent was bouncing all over the place but held up quite well.

It never did rain but we got lots of thunder and lightning. I was in my tent with everything closed up trying to keep the dust out and listening to the wind when I heard a series of "ohs and ahs" which sounded exactly like the 4th of July. Someone came to tell me that we were having an impressive display of lightning. Luckily it all went to the south of us and, other than a flurry of raindrops that caused everyone to run for cover, we got no rain. The wind blew until quite late, making it difficult to get to sleep, even though I was exhausted and so sleepy I couldn't read.

(Mike Mitchell #1) This was a really fun day for me. I woke up feeling really good and strong. As usual I was one of the first people up. I don't know why but I decided to see if today I could be one of the first three riders to get to camp. I was too early for breakfast but as soon as the light was up I headed out. I got into a good rhythm and picked up a small tailwind. I stopped and had a quick breakfast at the first place open and then got right back on the bike and pushed. After about an hour I came to a road construction stop. The lady on the sign said that they were just getting ready to move some large equipment down the road and it could be two hours or more before I would be able to pass. Two hours meant that I would be caught by a lot of the riders and so much for my early arrival at camp. I decided to tell a little white lie and see

If I could move on. I told the lady that I was in a race, that there were 299 riders behind me and that if she held me there I would lose my lead. I said you can see by my bike number #1 that I am the leader. I said I'm one of the oldest riders in the group so this was really important to me. She said "let me see what I can do" she got on her radio and I heard her say "have you started down the road yet? I have one cyclist I would like to let through before you get going" In a few seconds the reply came back "let him come". I got a big smile on my face and I thanked her very much. As I got down the road I made sure to wave and thank every truck I went by. This two hour lead insured my being first into camp. I even beat the support truck with our gear by about 20 minutes. I learned the negative part of getting to camp early is that when any work needs to be done like unloading something they don't hesitate asking for your help which of course you give. I spent several hours helping but was still proud of my effort for the day. I think God has a sense of humor and forgave my white lie.

(Nancy Eiselt #6) Today was a challenging ride. Strong winds of 20-25 mph fought us all day. There were cross winds, not headwinds, but tiring nonetheless. By afternoon the temperature was in the 90's and the radiated heat from the asphalt made it warmer. The final 20 miles to camp here at Poplar HS were darned tough, but I just kept thinking it could have been worse (we could have ridden 100 miles instead of 68, it could've been 110 degrees out - as it was last year - and the winds could have been real headwinds.)

(Marianne Brems #49) Today was a hot windy day that drove the spirit down more than it fatigued the body. The river at the end was a religious experience.

I've never felt wind like that before. It was as if the air had a mind of it's own. It was sort of like the force and fury of the water. It takes you in it's arms and has no mercy.

They say that the bonding begins when the going gets tough. Robin says she saw more hugging going on today. I think we are still to close to the adversity of the day to realize the bonds. I think it will sneak up on us and suddenly we will realize it's there and laugh or cry about it.

An electrical storm is somehow more dramatic without rain. The Trekker's were excited and cheering like at a football game with every bolt of lightning the cheers went up. Then a man presumably from the Chamber of Commerce went around the track in a pick-up truck full of popsicles yelling "popsicles, get your popsicles here".

Chapter 4

Day 16 Poplar Montana to Williston North Dakota 69 miles as remembered by Trekkers **Guy Smith #280, Mary Fleming #27, Nancy Ackles #124, Ellen Lowe #42 and Marianne Brems #49**

NOTE: *Julianne McKinney # 155 and Twinky McKinney # 13 were the only sister team on the trek.*

(Nancy Ackles #124) Nancy said, "It's amazing how when you pass from Montana into North Dakota, the bars give way to bakeries.

(Guy Smith #280) On Monday morning, everyone realized right away that something had changed. The wind was blowing strong, but the direction had shifted to the Southeast. Very quickly we learned the significance of a quartering head wind - it not only slowed us down but also blew the bike sideways into the roadway, requiring the cyclist to lean into the wind. I had agreed to ride with Sheri from Minneapolis, known as the Trekker mystic, because I wanted to chat with her. However, with the wind howling round our ears it was impossible to hold a conversation. The only relief was to ride almost abreast sheltering each other from the wind. Methodically we switched the lead every mile. The temperature soared in the 100's and we couldn't drink enough water. Stopping at every opportunity, Trekkers sat on the lee side of any structure, stores, houses or cafes to get some temporary relief from the wind. The route followed the Missouri river through the huge Fort Peck Indian Reservation. At Wolf Point we chatted with some Indians who had traveled to be there for a Pow-Wow. One named "Grayback" gave Sheri a $2.00 donation from his tribe to the American Lung Association, a significant gesture because they were all very poor. Our destination Poplar, could be seen in the distance, a typical Montana town with grain elevators and a green water tower. Several hours later it was still there in the distance, seemingly further away - perhaps a mirage. Finally we arrived; many felt this was the toughest day of the Trek. My toughest was yet to come. The highlight of the evening was a huge thunder storm which surrounded us, but no rain fell on our camp. The wind howled across the Poplar High school football field turned into a tent city, and those who didn't stake down their tents had to chase them as they danced around wildly. In the darkness Trekkers cheered the powerful lightning show like it was a fireworks display. That day I had to get my bicycle pedals replaced because the bearings were making a clicking sound. On the Trek there were three bike mechanics who worked out of a transformed Budget rental truck. They were the best in the business and often worked through the night performing miracles on ailing bicycles, Without Jose, Craig and Duane some of us would still be on the plains of Montana.

(Mary Fleming #27) I woke up at 4:30 a.m. to light clouds and no winds. I was afraid that it wouldn't last so I packed up, had breakfast and got on the road before 6:00 a.m. We had a very light tailwind for an hour or so then it picked up. Later in the day it became more northerly but never caused much of a problem. My legs were very tired from yesterday and uphill was a real effort.

The prairies just keep stretching on. We left the Fort Peck Indian reservation at 30 miles. The Indians that I talked to were all very nice and friendly and quite curious about the trip. We entered North Dakota after 57 miles and 10 days of traveling in Montana.

I made pretty good time today, though I was tiring significantly by the last 20 miles. Possible due to my sore thighs and bottom, I did something wrong today and have developed a pain in my Achilles tendon. Tomorrow we have a day of rest. We are actually staying in a hotel for two nights. I am rooming with Bonnie Hanlon #277.

I'm not sure yet what there is to do here. I am very sleepy right now and we haven't even had dinner yet, Maybe I'll have another day of reading. That really sounds appealing. Without the effects of yesterday still hanging on, today would have been a great day. Our next riding day will be 75 miles to New Town, North Dakota.

(Ellen Lowe #42) I remember the luxury of sleeping in a Trek provided motel room in Williston. The idea of not putting up or taking down the tent was pure bliss. I'm not sure which was the bigger thrill, the softness of the mattress or the fact that the bathroom was close by with NO long line.

Day 17 Williston North Dakota Rest Day as remembered by Trekkers Guy Smith #280, Mary Fleming #27, Roger Whidden # 190, Nancy Ackles #124 and Marianne Brems #49

(Marianne Brems #49) Staying in a hotel room all day was an experience almost foreign. I could talk on the phone and spread my assignment out on the table. It's a neat assignment. The number of ways to present an idea never ceases to amaze me. To be alone all day was a new experience. I don't want to camp ever again.

BIO NANCY ACKLES #124

Why did I decide to go on the Trek? Well, I had not heard of the ride, but someone suggested it to my friend Suzzane. That night we and our husbands had dinner together, she said, "Hey Nancy, want to ride across the United States?" I felt something well up inside me that said "Yes". Was it because when I was young I'd fantasized about walking across the US? I don't know, but that yes welled up, and I decided to go. Then when Suzzane decided she couldn't go along, I was on my own. I didn't know anyone else on the ride, all my previous cycling had included my husband and sometimes my children. This time they stayed home and rooted for me. I'm glad I went.

(**Nancy Ackles # 124**) My best day was leaving Williston just because we rode through such empty country. I remember passing a few farm houses as we left town because I was hoping to see the home of one of my older fiends in Seattle. I didn't find it. The rest of the day, I didn't see buildings just fields. We couldn't have been that far from communities because at one point we passed along the back of a golf course, and some women on golf carts lined up to wave to us, but we didn't see a club house or any other kind of house either. At check point, the support staff had bread and peanut butter and raisins available because there wasn't anyplace to buy food, and I sat in the sun and wind eating and enjoying the day. I could ride along empty roads and feel like a kid set free. It was for me, an empty, beautiful day.

(**Guy Smith #280**) Williston was the site of our second rest day, and we were spoiled there. The Trek had rented most of the Airport International Inn so we had beds and phones for two nights and full hotel facilities including a pool and sauna. We invaded the hotel lounge that evening and staged a wild toga party, the likes of which had never been seen in North Dakota before. I shared a room with Gary from California, who later in the Trek received the snoring championship award. I got a blast of his musical tunes when I left the Toga party; immediately I was missing my tent. The layover day in Williston was a lazy one. I did some laundry, shopping, chatting, bike cleaning and saw a movie. I never once

North Dakota

got on the bike.

(Mary Fleming #27) Had a very lazy day. Received mail yesterday, which was nice. Eddie and Cindy sent me a card and some Ginseng Tea for energy and medication for sore muscles. both very appropriate. Mom sent a postcard of the North Coast Sea Shore (I'm going to attach it to my handlebar pack for hot days) and a supply of cookies and hard candies. (I guess I will just have to delay my food reduction, which I had planned for the rest day, Too bad!!)

(Roger Whidden #190) Mass start from hotel (after toga party)to New Town. Small group racing beautiful country of gently winding hills and minimal traffic.Choice point! Am I going to try to catch the leader Scott, or play it safe and ride with the pack? I go for it - feel like my heart is going to explode and my lungs are on fire. I catch him, we jockey for 20 miles or so then vow to catch the guy who left one hour earlier (obsessed with being the first one to camp everyday) we catch him, he tries to hang - then we mercilessly drop him - animals that we are - later in Trek I experience going from animal to cannibal never knew that capability existed.

Day 18 Williston North Dakota to New Town North Dakota 75 miles as remembered by Trekkers Mike Mitchell #1, Guy Smith #280, Mary Fleming #27, Ellen Lowe #42 and Marianne Brems # 49

(Mike Mitchell #1) This is one day I wouldn't forget. Prior to leaving for Trek I had a couple of bouts with Kidney Stones and I knew when I left that I still had some. Now Kidney Stones can stay in your Kidney's for years and not move or they can move around as fast as you make them. The doctor told me that riding a bike with the jarring around and everything else, that there was a good chance I would pass some stones on the trip. Well for the last couple of days I had been having some pain in the kidney area and sure enough that day the pain built up to where I knew something had to give. I told staff what was going on and at the end of the day they tried to help me check into a motel so I would be more comfortable that night. As it turns out there had been only one room

67

available and a Trekker had taken it. When staff asked him to let me have it he refused so that night in my tent "Rocky 1" was born or passed whichever way you look at it. I picked up a small pebble in the morning put it in a box with some cotton and after that when I checked in I signed in as Trekker #1 and Rocky #1. Rocky rode the rest of the way to Atlantic City where I threw him in the ocean. (Since that time his brother's and sister's have grown to over 200. Wish they were valuable stones, I would be a millionaire.)

(Guy Smith #280) Today we left Williston in a parade. Ordinarily bikers leave camp at their own pace with the earliest starting at dawn (before 5:00 a.m.) and the last folks, getting on the road around 9:30 a.m. But this morning was special; the city had closed the eastbound lanes of the highway and we rode out of town in a parade of 300 bicyclists with all of our support vehicles. It was part of the celebration of the 100th anniversary of North Dakota's statehood. Not many locals were up that early to witness our departure, but it was a great sight to see the line of bicycles climbing the steep hill just east of town. We had sadly left Stace from Wisconsin in a hospital at Williston, she had gone horseback riding on our off day and fell when the cinch broke, breaking her elbow. Up to this point, all of the Trekkers who started in Seattle had stayed with it. The morning was slightly cool with almost no wind, but riding the gentle hills along the Missouri River quickly warmed us up. At the checkpoint the staff provided us with lunch, because there were no cafes or food stores for miles, ordinarily we bought our own lunch or carried food with us. I had my first peanut butter and raisin sandwich. Try it! Our destination, New Town was recently developed to replace two Indian towns that were flooded by the waters of Lake Sakakawea when the Garrison Dam was built on the Missouri River. It is in the Fort Berthold Indian Reservation, and the Indians treated us to a Pow Wow with authentic songs and dances and invited us to join in the ceremony. < Insert picture #17> An old Indian woman offered an inspirational prayer asking God to protect the bicyclists on the road and to keep us away from drivers who are careless with human life. Her prayer was a prophecy. The Indians had erected some authentic tepees among our tents on the grounds of the New Town High School and some Trekkers slept in them. It was a very noisy night with many locals driving by and whooping it up. In the morning two bicycles were missing and the two victims. Becky and Lindy, had to ride staff mountain bikes that day. This story has a happy ending, as both bikes were recovered the same day when two boys tried to sell them at a bike shop in the nearby town of Minot.

(Mary Fleming #27) After a day of rest I woke up at 5:00 a.m., got packed, loaded my gear, ate breakfast, brought my bike down and checked out of the hotel. By the time I finished all of this it was about 6:00a.m. We were scheduled to leave at 7 a.m. as a parade with all of the cyclists and all of the support vehicles. I spent some time catching up on the TV news.

AT 6:45 a.m.we all assembled for photo's and at 7:00 a.m. we were on the road. We were quite a spectacle and there were a surprising number of people out to wish us well, considering the hour of the morning. We made a parade of about 1 mile in length, using both driving lanes.

The only stop today was at a Marina which had a pretty limited supply of food and drink. Even the checkpoint was out in the middle of nowhere. In spite of the fact that everyone started at 7 a.m. people seemed to be just as spread out as ever, with some arriving before noon and others late afternoon.

New Town is apparently within an Indian reservation. We got a tour to the Marina and to the Indian cultural museum. The trip today was relatively easy, with gently rolling hills and cool weather. I cut back a little on the eating.

(Ellen Lowe #42) I remember the shock of learning North Dakota is NOT flat. Purely against all bicycling rules of the road, we learned we could ride four abreast and not encounter a car for hours at a time. We also learned we could get train engineers to blow their train whistles simple by waving and a pull down hand/arm motion.

(Marianne Brems #49) Five women in golf carts all smiling appeared on the side of the road without warning. Where in the world did they come from?

Everything today was funny. I had a water bottle fight with Robin and we wrote on each other like grade school children. I decided that being on Trek is akin to being in prison in the sense that we are a more or less a captive community.

The Indian dancing left me a little sad because I wished that I knew more about it's significance. The songs sounded all the same to me. Sleeping in a tepee was a new experience.

Day 19 New Town ND to Max ND 75 miles as remembered by Trekkers Guy Smith #280, Mary Fleming #27, Hal Laster #16, Nancy Eiselt #6, Nancy Ackles #124 and Marianne Brems #49

NOTE: *Will Decker # 35 and Bill Decker #45 were the only father-son team on the Trek.*

(Nancy Ackles #124) A special memory I have this day is the children who came to visit me in my tent, so polite. We shared granola bars and water, and they ran home to get permission to stay a few minutes longer and bring me a yogurt pushup. Our sea of tents was just as fascinating to them as the local tepee was to the Trekkers.

BIO HAL LASTER #16

In 1989 I was a student at the University of Cincinnati College-Conservatory of music. I was truly a novice cyclist. A close high school friend had ridden solo from Tacoma WA to Yorktown, VA when he retired from the Army.... And to be quite truthful I thought he was totally out of his mind. A year later, a student at the University asked me if I had ever thought of bicycling cross-country, and I gave him the same response your crazy. That conversation was on a Wednesday night following a concert, and by Friday, I had bought a bicycle helmet, gloves, cycling shorts and different shoes, got on my son's bicycle Saturday morning and rode 26 miles on the Loveland Bicycle Trail just outside Cincinnati, and I remember saying to myself while thinking of a cross country ride "I can do this" the rest is history!!

Not only did I ride 1989 from Seattle to Atlantic City, but I did it again five years later in 1994 - Los Angeles to Orlando (or Disney to Disney) And I can honestly state that those two phenomenal trips (as well as a North/South ride from Portland, ME to Orland FL in 1990, and two weeks of solo cycling in France in 1992) totally changed my life. And not a day goes by that I don't fail to reflect in someway about one of those rides.

(Hal Laster #16) Were there rough days? Yes. A Montana headwind of 25 mph: three consecutive days averaging over 100 miles each day: traffic in the major cities of Minneapolis, Milwaukee and Chicago, the Appalachian Mountains in Pennsylvania. Today I was slower than usual due to winds (and not the tail wind type either), and the later it got, the heavier the head-wind became. I was truly struggling. I remember counting along the side of the road, pedal strokes, just to get my mind off the wind. I was grateful that Don Baer rode back to meet me and help "pull me in". He was the best riding buddy anyone could have ever asked for!!

There were also days filed with happiness; going 49 mph downhill after the Steven's Pass climb, daily stops along the route with kids who had prepared lemonade and kool-aid stands for us,seeing small town America at it's best (and some small towns perhaps at their worst)stopping at Dairy Queen's for Butterscotch milkshakes, partying and relaxing on our five off days and the Trekker celebration in the Atlantic Ocean on July 21.

(Guy Smith #280) June 23rd was a day some of us had been waiting for - Michelle's 24th birthday. She wanted to keep it secret because Trekkers make a big deal about birthdays and Michelle was bashful about it. Early that morning in New Town, while Michelle was conversing with a deaf Indian in sign language; Lori her best friend from California, and I prepared a sign. As we rode out I secretly tacked the sign to the back of her bike announcing in large letters, "IT'S MY BIRTHDAY'. She was puzzled at all the birthday greetings she got from everyone along the road. I had a moment of panic when she stopped to take off her jacket, but I managed to pull the sign off and then replace it when we rode on. She began to get suspicious when four guys sang 'Happy Birthday" to her; she didn't even know them I finally got caught. But she enjoyed the joke and even wore her sign into the mid-day checkpoint at Makoti. Arriving there she couldn't hide her birthday any longer. Lori had ridden ahead and arranged a big sign to announce the day. Makoti, ND is a very special town; the people there love the Transamerica Trek and extended themselves to welcome us. A troop of clowns and a costumed jackass greeted us along the road. In the city park the townsfolk had fabulous goodies and nice signs to welcome us. Michelle and I spent a long time there touring the grain elevators, barns full of old fashioned farm equipment and even a miniature Midwest village. In the old school house I found two primers I had used in grammar school and even found pictures and stories I remembered in "Street and Roads". We felt so welcome in Makoti, a town that helped to reinforce the idea that people of North Dakota were the nicest we met across the USA. It was late afternoon when we rode into Max, and by the time our 300 trekkers and staff arrived we doubled the size of the town.

(Mary Fleming #27) Today was a very gentle and not particularly difficult ride. A lot of the terrain was level or gently rising. There didn't seem to be much downhill. There was minimal wind until late in the ride and it was cloudy and cool, ideal riding conditions under most circumstances.

I started out tired but feeling fairly strong. After about 15 miles, my Achilles tendon began to hurt quite badly and I found that I was pedaling almost entirely with my right leg. I stopped and spent some time massaging the tendon area and it felt quite a bit better. My bottom is hurting a lot lately. It seems to be bones making contact with the seat. I will try to add some more padding tomorrow.

We camped at the local school. Our checkpoint was at Makoti, which is where they have spent the night in previous years. The people were apparently disappointed to lose us, as we were a big event for them. We were met out at the highway by a group of clowns and a mule. A big welcome sign and a package of souvenir wheat.

They provided us with food and drinks. The town also had a museum of threshing equipment, steam engines and some typical structures such as a one room school house, a homestead shack, a church, a post office/drugstore and a blacksmith shop.

North Dakota seems much more populated than Montana. Most farm houses have trees planted around them and as you ride you can always see several homes from the road. The land is farmed more often than ranched. There is also oil in the area. I saw some active wells and at least one drilling rig. Our route passed several abandoned farmhouses.

You can clearly see what weather is approaching for quite some time. That is, if you look in the right direction. Several of us got caught in a thunder storm and took shelter in an abandoned farmhouse. The terrain, though gently rolling, seems to be on a plain that is sloped up to the east.

(Nancy Eiselt #6) Although the weather was beautiful today, I didn't enjoy it as much as most of the others. I had my mind more fixed on reaching my destination than on enjoying the ride today, for some reason. I think I was concerned about facing headwinds, so I got going earlier than I have in a long time (6 a.m.) and rode fairly hard all the way to Makoti.

I found that a lot of people had a less-than-terrific day today. I think we're beginning to tire of the routine now: the charm and magic aren't as apparent and even though we've had fabulous riding conditions, were beginning to see that we're doing very much the "same old thing" each day. It's good for me to realize that no matter what I'm doing, if I let it become routine, I begin to tire of it. My challenge will be to take a fresh look at the day/ride each day and continue to see the adventure in it.

(Marianne Brems #49) Visiting Makoti was like something from fantasy land. Pat whose husband owns a grain elevator was like a pig in a swill, sitting on the tractor that was running. The population of the town more than doubled with our arrival. They loved having us even though only for a checkpoint, not overnight. They were disappointed when we did not plan to spend the night there this year.

I'll never forget seeing the banner on the side of the road "Go Go Marianne Brems" and the letter with it saying that I was an Olympic champion. This was from the Assistant Probation Officer of San Mateo County.

I ate a cheese sandwich at the Centennial Café that cost 85

cents. Hearing Garrison Kellor (the scenario about having the flu) laughing ourselves silly until tears ran down was the highlight of the day.

Day 20 Max North Dakota to Harvey North Dakota 77 miles as remembered by Trekkers Guy Smith #280, Mary Fleming #27, Virgil Kemp #154, Nancy Eiselt #6 and Marianne Brems #49

(Guy Smith #280) Saturday was cool and overcast most of the day; it was a real luxury to wear long sleeved shirts and to get a reprieve from the searing sun. I rode with Karin at a leisurely pace preferring to enjoy the rural towns rather than hurrying along. In a café at Butte a local man named Ted was exuberant about the bicycle Trek and announced that he would pay for breakfast for all the Trekker's who came in. But he didn't know about the intricate communication network we had. Within minutes the word spread down the road, and the quiet little café was jammed full of excited people ordering homemade pie and pecan rolls. Poor Ted was overwhelmed and had to limit his offer to 30 people. In the town of Martin, we met an old man who boasted of his harmonica skills, so we invited him to come to Harvey to meet 68 year old Lou, the Trekker harmonica wizard. That night we were treated to a duet sing along that extended into the night. Lou was excited to meet the old guy and though neither one could hardly hear, their music and fun was a Trek highlight. A couple of us slipped away to go to Mass at St. Cecilia's. During his sermon the local pastor gave intricate details of everything going on in town, better than the town newspaper. He welcomed us several times and asked the congregation to pray for our safe journey.

(Mary Fleming #27) I saw Wendy, one of our EMT's last night about my sore ankle. She assured me that it is my Achilles tendon that is hurting and gave me some stretches for the calf, told me to ice it at checkpoint and at the end of the day and to get it taped before leaving today. I did all of the above and felt no pain today.

(Virgil Kemp #154) I was expecting numerous days with tailwinds, riding West to East. But,guess what? The prevailing winds in Northwest on Route 2 are from the East. We had 4-5 days of 100 to 115 miles with headwinds? It was really flat in North Dakota and Minnesota, etc. with no place to hide from the wind. I personally would rather have wind than mountains any day, but the wind in that area is brutal.Strong and hot. Those were hard days.

(Nancy Eiselt #6) We've been on the road long enough now that certain simple things are being recognized as real gifts and pleasures; flush toilets, level ground on which to pitch a tent, oatmeal for breakfast, anything other than pasta for dinner, time to do "real" laundry.... I'm beginning to worry about how I'll cope with the former everyday concerns like bills, household upkeep, work schedule etc.

Day 22 Cooperstown North Dakota to Moorhead Minnesota 97 miles as remembered by Trekkers Guy Smith #280, Mary Fleming #27 and Marianne Brems #49

(Guy Smith #280) I was off to a bad start this morning with a broken rear spoke which caused the wheel to wobble. Craig got me back on the road again and I hitched up with Shelley from Los Angeles and Marty from Georgia. Once again the westerly winds were in our favor, but the very rough road was tough on our behinds so early in the morning. The terrain was flat as a table top and for miles we could see the KTHI-TV Tower at 2063 feet, the worlds tallest structure. Trees became more plentiful, outlining lush green fields of corn, sunflowers and wheat. Marty and I had a race and hammered along at 31 mph, really fast for a level road. But it was Shelly's bike that broke a spoke under the strain, and we again witnessed the ability of the bike mechanics crew to get her rolling. Fargo ND was the first city we had seen since Spokane WA, city streets and traffic sharply reminded us that the peace and tranquility of the West was being left behind. We crossed the Red River into Minnesota our fifth state and were treated to a real bed in Nelson Hall at Moorhead State University.

Sunrise 47

(**Mary Fleming #27**) We camped in the city park at Cooperstown and were served our meals in the fairgrounds. Either the food on this trip is exceptionally good for mass feeding or I am just so hungry that anything would taste good. Dinner was salad and either BBQ beef sandwiches or grilled cheese. Breakfast was oatmeal, muffins, fruit, French toast and pancakes.

    I was so tired, that I had made up my mind to only ride part way. Jim decided to ride with me and then provided encouragement and pressure to complete the whole day. Luckily it was an easy day to ride 96 miles. We had a strong wind from the west which was directly behind us most of the time, at a 45 degree angel some of the time and a crosswind briefly. We were doing a real easy 18-19 mph when it was directly behind us. It was a drag as a crosswind but an average of 10 mph including some breaks is pretty good for me.

The further east we got in North Dakota, the more trees we saw other than those around the farmhouse. The farms look more and more prosperous and spiffy.

Coming into Fargo N.D. was a shock. We paralleled a major interstate highway with all of it's noise and saw a skyline of multi-story structures for the first time in many days. The tallest structures we have seen lately were grain elevators and water towers. We were arriving at commute time so the traffic on the downtown streets was heavy and we really had to focus on how to ride in traffic all over again. We are used to having the road to ourselves for ten miles at a time.

I tried to call Mom's cousin, Donald McMillan, who teaches at Moorhead, but he works evenings and wasn't there. I was just going to say hello.

There was an Army jazz band for us over at the dinner hall. I thought that was really nice. I was going to try to catch the shuttle to see Batman but didn't move fast enough. Some people went ice skating tonight. I hope we don't have any injuries. One of the girls Stacey, fell off a horse in Williston and shattered her elbow.

(Marianne Brems #49) The feeling that we'll be halfway tomorrow is weighing heavy. I can't imagine going back and having to perform as a leader two days after I return.

We really are in a time warp. We left three weeks ago today. In a way it seems like a thousand years ago and in another sense it seems like yesterday. I like looking at the dates on my Tyvek jacket because they are still active. July 21st hasn't arrived yet. Usually when you get a t-shirt by the time you put it on the date has passed.

Chapter 5

Day 23 Moorehead ND to Alexandria MN 107 miles as remembered by Trekker Guy Smith #280, Nancy Ackles #124, Mike Mitchell #1 and Marianne Brems #49

(**Nancy Ackles #124**) Nancy said, "I remember the cafeteria workers who said they didn't need to see Trekker ID to let us in to eat. They could tell who we were by our weird tan lines."

(**Guy Smith #280**) This morning started off cool with light tail winds, and I was on the road by 5:30 a.m. This was our longest day of the Trek, 107.4 miles. I saw a pace line up ahead moving at a nice easy tempo so I asked if I could join up. Then I realized it was Jim and Gerry from Washington, Cindy from Alaska and Marian from Massachusetts, also know as "Team Damn Good". They were just warming up. These four riders were way beyond my ability; but I thought it would be fun to ride with them, at least until they got warmed up. Almost undetectably the pace quickened until we were dashing up and down the rolling hills of Western Minnesota at 18-23 mph. In a pace line each person takes their turn up front, breaking the wind for the others who have an easier ride if they hold a position about one foot behind the bike in front of them. It's a very intense disciplined ride; not much chance to do sight seeing. I was challenging every muscle in my body when I was in the lead and every ounce of concentration when I rode in the pack. If you get even a few feet behind, it's murder to catch up again. No wonder I was wolfing down my first snack of the day by 7:00 a.m. Team Damn Good knew how to enjoy themselves too, so we stopped to enjoy the sights like the huge "Prairie Chicken" statue in Barnesville. I stayed with them, pushing myself to the mid-day checkpoint at Fergus Falls. There I did a radio interview for a local station and rested. When the team got on the road again, like a maniac I went along. We pounded along to Ashley on Pelican Lake where we celebrated another major milestone, the halfway point of the Trek. I fueled up on melons and milk shakes and continued on with "team damn good", though my body was screaming at me to stop this madness. But now I wanted to prove to myself that I could ride the longest day with the fastest team. We had a near disaster when I was leading the pace line, the fastener on my Blackburn rack broke, slamming the rack with the two panniers (saddle bags) against my rear tire. Acting like a brake it slowed me down immediately with out warning. Such an occurrence would normally cause a pileup of 5 bikes. But the reactions and split second decisions of the four riders of "team damn good" proved that they deserved their names. With a lot of yells and some tricky riding all five of us came to a stop without mishap. I fixed the rack, but they refused to let me ride lead anymore. I don't blame them. Despite all the stops and interruptions we arrived at Alexandria at 1:20 p.m. My body was quivering and my brain couldn't function enough to put my tent up. So I walked to Dairy Queen with Joy from NJ to recuperate in the air conditioning with an extra big

Blizzard. Walking back to camp on the grounds of the Central Junior High School, a strange thing happened to us as we crossed the street. A car approached and suddenly veered across the median. It looked like the driver was intentionally trying to hit us. I gripped Joy and pulled her to the safety of the sidewalk. The car door opened and out jumped my brother Pete. With this strange greeting I began my second visit of the Trek with Pete, Sue, and Barron. They enjoyed dinner with us, took a swim in the school pool and camped with us in tent city. Pete thrilled five of the Trekkers with a flight in his Piper Seneca to view the Trek from different perspective. Though I was totally exhausted it was difficult to sleep that night because of the heat and too much artificial light at the school.

(Marianne Brems #49) It does as Garrison Kiellor said "seems as if we are a tiny speck to be swallowed by a bear and as large as the universe itself". It left me sad to reach halfway. I think the hardest part of all of this may be that we have to get there. I want to feel differently or I won't draw the strength from the experience that I need to have when I get home. I feel unwilling to go back to a life where I don't smell the roses.

(Mike Mitchell #1) The longest day of the Trek. A couple of significant things will happen today. We will leave the prairies and at Pelican Lake we will reach the halfway point for the Trek. Hard to believe that we have come this far already. Again as has become my pattern for the long days I broke it into segments and took a good half hour break in between. Riding alone most of the time thinking about my granddaughter and daughter. Wishing the ride would end soon but still trying to be caught up in the moment and enjoy the beauty and the friendships. Took a swim in the school pool and had a great dinner. The food has been absolutely fabulous with every town and group trying to outdo the last one.

Day 24 Alexandria Minnesota to St Cloud Minnesota 78 miles as remembered by Trekkers Guy Smith #280, Mary Fleming #27, and Marianne Brems #49

(Guy Smith #280) In the morning I was really dragging. After breakfast and a farewell to Pete and his family, I was off to a slow start with the Los Angeles gang: Ellen, Shelly and Kevin. Strong head winds didn't help, neither did the hills. Our group fell apart. First Shelley had a flat and Kevin stayed behind with her. Then Ellen stayed in Sauk Center, the home of Sinclair Lewis and the town where she was born. So I joined up with another group: Ali from Vermont, Tom from Washington, Sam from Rhode Island and Twinky from Connecticut. We called ourselves "Ali and the Cat's". Midday checkpoint came early in the ride at St. Rose's Catholic Church in St Rosa. In the church hall the ladies Society had prepared homemade treats for us. I ate to many sweet things, and at Holdingford, about 50 miles into the day I was flat. I started to hate my bike and couldn't find the strength to go on. Ali suggested a picnic so we all purchased something and put together a very relaxing picnic in the city park. We stretched out the break as long as we could, then returned to battling the heat, humidity and the head winds. That afternoon we came to the west bank of the Mississippi river and road along River Road which would be our route for the next three days. All five of us were dragging by the time we arrived at St. Cloud and camped at the spacious tree covered VA medical center. St. Cloud was our third rest day of the trip and for me it was especially welcome, coming at the end of my toughest day of the Trek. I chained my bike to the limb of a tree, and to some it appeared that I had lynched it.

(Mary Fleming #27) Today we really got into Minnesota. The first half of the day was basically a continuation of the level prairie land. Long straight roads, flat and level land with lots of row crops. There were many more trees than previous days, not just around the farms, but apparently growing at random. We began to see a lot of lakes as we entered the hill country. As the day progresses there were more and more hills, not large hills, but scenic hills. The towns here, instead of being 20 to 40 miles apart, are 5 to 8 miles apart.

I woke up after not sleeping very well, feeling really tired and dreading 107 miles, as tired and sore as I was. I fully intended to catch the sag wag for at least the first half of the day and maybe the whole day. Somehow I found myself going through the preparations for riding, just in case I decided to do a partial ride, and all of a sudden I found myself on the bicycle pedaling down the road. The force of habit is very strong and the extra effort required to line up a ride seemed excessive.

I rode very slow for 15 miles until I came to the first van. I was very sore, hands and bottom, and just worn out. I thought some energy might turn up after awhile, but it never did so I sagged from there. I ended up explaining and justifying the rest of the day. Everybody always seems so concerned if they know that you accepted a ride.

I intended to be in bed by 8:30 tonight and up early enough to leave by 6:30 a.m. It was hot today and hopefully I can avoid some of the heat tomorrow with this tactic.

(Marianne Brems #49) Consumerism and a whole wall full of transistor radios seem out of place when we have been through towns where there's little more than a pay phone. I asked the checkout girl if she knew who we were and she looked at me as if to say "no and I don't want to know". We are in the big city compared to the muffins, cookies and lemonade for the better part of the day from the Lions Club and the church. It was strange to go to a movie and have no home to go to afterwards.

Day 25 St Cloud Minnesota rest day 0 miles as remembered by Trekkers Guy Smith #280, Mary Fleming #27, Ellen Lowe #42 Marianne Brems #49 and Karin Allen #29

(Ellen Lowe #42) I remember what a stir I caused passing trough my home town of Sauk Centre. MN. A reporter from the Sauk Centre Herald met Shelley and I at the end of main street for a quick interview. The following day we were headline news "Harry Huston's daughter cycles for ALA". In 1955, when I was 8 years old, our family moved from MN to CA. yet this small dairy/farm community honored my Dad with our human interest story 25 years after he had passed away. My brother, Dale flew to MN for a huge Huston Family Reunion. I was able to show my city-girl, Shelley, the farm where I was born, took her up into the hay loft and introduced her to hay balers, tractors and even a few cows.

(Marianne Brems #49) I got un-trekked today in an appalling hurry. I worked on my lesson for six hours and did some good work, even in a noisy room. It always surprises me when people walk in turn on the TV and then leave without turning it off.

(Karin Allen #29) Rest day! This day was particularly memorable because we went to see the movie "Dead Poet's Society". It was amazing how much this movie resonated with us, as the big line is "Carpe Diem" which means, "Seize the Day". If there was something I had really come to appreciate as a Trekker was the idea that you really need to live life to the fullest, seize the day, and make the most of your short time here on Earth.

(Guy Smith #280) On Thursday our rest day, I slept late (to 7:30 a.m.) and spent the day resting, doing laundry and sitting in air conditioned movie theaters with wide cushioned seats. Among the many "Trekker Treats" we enjoyed there, a nearby shopping plaza theater gave us free admission to the movies throughout the day.

(Mary Fleming #27) St Cloud is a lovely town along the Mississippi river. I wandered around town to look around for awhile. They have a nice mall in the old area where they have closed off the street and created a pedestrian mall and set up a few sculptures, planters and benches. There was a nice park along the edge of the river that seemed to be heavily used, even on a week day.

We stayed at the local VA medical center and ate at their cafeteria.

Day 26 StCloud Minnesota to Minneapolis Minnesota 80 miles as remembered by Trekkers Guy Smith #280, Virgil Kemp #154, Mary Fleming #27, Roger Whidden #190 and Marianne Brems #49

(Guy Smith #280) Friday morning started with a bang; thunder and lightning and a very wet tent. I couldn't go back to sleep anyway, so I started packing my things, even though it was still quite dark. Others had the same idea and just as daybreak arrived, I met with Karin, Nancy and Terri who were not intimidated by the storm. We started out without breakfast (it was still to early), protected only by our rain gear. Our route took us along small county roads sandwiched between 2 major interstate highways, so there was virtually no traffic on our road. After 15 miles of early biking our appetites were ready for the huge muffins and caramel rolls we found at a truck stop bakery. We passed the word to bikers behind us, and soon the place was jammed - a real "Trekker Trap". The rain let up later in the morning and the sun even warmed us up in the afternoon. Passing through Anoka, the "Halloween Capital of the World" we were treated to free lemonade and fruit. This town has a week long celebration of Halloween, a custom created to replace pranks and violence with creative fun. Large pumpkin signs and buttons proudly proclaim this to visitors. Approaching Minneapolis from the north didn't give us the best view of the city, only later when I took a drive with an old Navy friend to their house in the suburbs did I realize what a beautiful city it really is. Covered with lakes, parks and beautiful homes, it seems like a great place to live. We stayed in the dorms of Augsburg College, a Lutheran school, but I couldn't sleep well because of the intense heat and humidity.

(Virgil Kemp #154) After doing Transamerica in 1987 I had a jump on doing Transamerica for 1989. So I was able to start a scientific research project I had been planning from the first day. No one else would ask this question or seek the answer. It was up to me to seek out the answer by purely scientific means, for generations that would live with commercialization of even our simplest basic needs. My test results would reflect a time of quality when workmanship was more important than disposable, cookie-cutter, nothing is real (look at the ingredients on a label) and everything tastes the same.

By now you know I was going to sacrifice my personal well-being to find the best chocolate malt in these United States of America. As part of my research I committed to consuming at least 2 or more chocolate malts a day. But scientific research being what it is I needed criteria, parameters and qualifying objectives.

First of all the malt had to be a one of a kind preparation, not made by a machine. Handmade or homemade if you may was paramount. I knew from preliminary investigations and extensive

Sunrise 47

background that fast food places were not in the running. Handmade or homemade chocolate malts are served in a metal container with an accompanying glass. So there we have it - I was on a mission to find the best chocolate malt (not a shake) in America, made by hand and served in a metal container with an accompanying glass.

And so you are asking after I had committed myself to this self-imposed goal for future humanity while subjecting myself to the unknown. What did I find? The answer is "Annie's in Minneapolis". Granted I had done some preliminary research in "87" so I knew Annie's met the criteria. I had informed all my fellow Trekkers and my enthusiasm was picked up by the editor of our Trekker newsletter. "Go to Annie's in Minneapolis" per my recommendation.

So here we are at Annie's a large group of Trekkers yukking it up and of course I order a chocolate malt. I'm drinking the malt and it's great but a little different than I remember it so I mentioned it to the waiter. We then determined I got a special malt with a banana in it. He asked me if that is what I ordered and I said 'no" Well it turns out, restaurant policy says I can get another malt with no banana. Then he asks me the big question" do I want another malt"? Wow. This is a big point in my human endeavor for mankind can I endure the sacrifice so others may learn. That was the closest I came to a serious risk but I was able to ride the next day. As I look back on it now I'm glad I choose the 2nd malt because without it I couldn't have been able to name Annie's as the best chocolate malt in the USA as per "The Virg".

I am glad I did this research when I did because I believe with my whole heart it could not be completed today with the criteria and guidelines I used. I do not suffer any ill affects from the research, mainly because I kept my eye on the ball, spent years in training (I was no amateur) resisted temptations and my results are 100% accurate and correct.

(Mary Fleming #27) The wind was blowing rally hard today. It was, primarily a cross wind but sometimes a head wind. The ride, though not all that long in miles, was a long hard ride. It was only slightly hilly but there were long stretches along a freeway which is not very pleasant. The weather is hot and muggy and, in spite of the wind, it seems to be really hazy. In the second half of the day we got back near the river, which was some improvement, if not physically, at least mentally.

I think most of us wished that the rest day had been in Minneapolis rather that St Cloud. We stayed at Augsburg college which, unfortunately did not seem to have air conditioning. Minneapolis is an interesting city and one I would have liked to have some time to explore a little more. I went downtown for awhile to see the skyway system. There is an area of several blocks that include both offices and retail centers and the blocks are connected with second level covered walkways. The shopping malls are open to the interior of the block with first and second story and in some cases, third story shopping and eating facilities.

I went to visit the local art museum which was really nice for a change of pace. There is a lot of downtown development or redevelopment going on in the city. Our Trek photographer gave us a slide show of some of the work that he has completed up to this point. He will compile his slide into a video show with music, at the end of the trip and make it available to all Trekkers. I think I will get one for free because of the amount of contributions I have raised. It was listed as one of the incentives.

There was another big party at one of the local restaurant/bars which was sponsored by local resident riders and their families.

(Roger Whidden #190) Steve and I tandem through winding gentle hills of Minnesota he has his feet up and having the ride of his life and I'm loving it too! Keep on Trekking Steve.

(Marianne Brems #49) It's quite incredible to take a nap, wake up and it's all still there. What en experience when being awake is better than being asleep. You wake up and feel so happy that it's a new day. I don't want to lose that.

Day 27 Minneapolis Minnesota to Wabasha Minnesota 86 miles as remembered by Trekkers Guy Smith #280, Mary Fleming #27, Sharon White #291 and Marianne Brems #49

(Guy Smith #280) By morning it had cooled a little, but the humidity was still oppressive, and it got worse as the sun rose higher. For quite a while I rode alone, enjoying the serenity of the Mississippi River and the hilly beauty of St. Paul, the Twin City. Our route to Wabasha was mostly southeast, crossing the Mississippi several times and sometimes riding along a major four lane highway. Soon I became aware that I was being followed by Lou, a 68 year old man who walks with bowed legs and a very noticeable limp. I slowed up for him. We rode together for awhile, and I was amazed at how he was able to maintain a very respectable pace. I will be a very fortunate man if I can repeat this trip when I'm 68. Lou is one of the hero's. At Hastings a huge barge, larger than an aircraft carrier, was being maneuvered under the bridge and around a bend in the river. At Red Wing, home of the famous Red Wing shoes, I joined up with Karin and we rode together along Lake Pepin, a very wide area of the river. The heat and humidity were getting the best of us. Some chose to go for a swim, but we opted to spend about two hours in an air conditioned pizza parlor.

Our bodies wanted to rebel when we emerged into the bright sunshine, but we forced them to finish the ride to the city park at Wabasha. That night we attended a Saturday evening mass and went to bed early. Finally I got a good nights sleep as it cooled off a lot in the evening.

(Mary Fleming #27) We rode through Minneapolis/St Paul this morning. I was up early because I did not want to deal with the city traffic. I managed to miss most of it but it was beginning to get heavy as I got out of town. We rode south along the Mississippi today to the little town of Wabasha. This is where we crossed the river. Tomorrow we go into Wisconsin.

The countryside is really pretty here but there is no incentive to take photographs because of the haziness. It was extremely hot and muggy all day and did not get very much better at night. In the areas where we were close to the river it didn't seem to feel quite so bad. There was very little breeze today. We camped in the city park, which is right across the street from a camp ground that was full of RV's and very noisy campers. We are definitely back in civilization again.

The town is a cute little town that is, in some ways reminiscent of home. Some of the older houses are being converted into cute little restaurants, shops and bed and breakfast accommodations. I wandered downtown after dark and was looking for a soda. There were a couple of bars and lots of Pepsi machines scattered around the main street. They provided the main points of light and color in the darkened little town. Dinner was in the camp area.

BIO SHARON WHITE #291

In 1989, I was a newly-graduated university student, majoring in journalism and just returning from a job as a sports reporter in Whistler, B.C. (a ski resort). Two summers before the American Trek, I cycled 1,400 miles solo from Vancouver to northern British Columbia and back and wanted another adventure, but this time an organized tour as my family was horrified, perhaps rightly so, at my solo efforts. At the time, the only organized bike tour across Canada was for Senior Citizens and at 29, I was a few decades short of the age limit. So I sought out other opportunities and learned about the Transamerica Trek through a news magazine show.

(Sharon White #291) There's something about celebrating your national holiday in another country. This may come as a surprise to Americans, but it has been said and even referenced in NBC's West Wing show that Canada has an inferiority complex when it comes to the United States. Personally, I don't know about the "inferiority" part, but our feelings towards the US are certainly "complex". We don't want to be Americans, but were constantly comparing ourselves to them. We hate the big box Americanization of Canada, yet it's widely accepted that save for hockey players, your not a star athlete or entertainer unless you've made it in the States. And we poke fun at American's who still think we live in igloos and eat harbor seals for dinner, yet we don't have a strong sense of nationalism to wage against or stars and stripes insecurities.

A few days after Canada Day and before the Fourth of July, I was discussing patriotism and its hard sell in Canada with my riding partner Jenny Dickey from Baltimore. We had just stopped to visit a Fourth of July homage - a house along the Trek route festooned in American Flags and U.S. memorabilia complete with the owners decked out from head to toe as Uncle and Aunt Sam. This was a pattern repeated for each holiday observance- Christmas, Valentines Day, Easter - and the couple had a photo album to prove it.

Jen and I were teaching and singing each others respective national anthems. Of course, from my years of watching American television and sports, I knew the Star Spangled Banner so in between chords Jen and I discussed our patriotism, or lack thereof. She was surprised that Canadians saw Americans as stalwart patriots - a loyalty often perceived as aggressiveness and falsely translated worldwide into xenophobia.

Canadians don't have the same sense of nationalism. I told her that while we don't know our own history well, we can rattle off the names of most of the 50 states and name more of the U.S. Presidents than Canadian Prime Ministers. Jennifer was still skeptical about my comparison of patriotism until I asked her if she had an American flag at home. "yes," she innocently responded as if having a flag was as typical as having running water.(Note; I have a Canadian flag now too).

Now, there are more Canadain flags flying on Canada day. That's why, back in 1989, there was something about celebrating my national holiday in another country, particularly the United States. Celebrating Canada Day with more than 300 Americans could have been very lonely, but thanks to the camaraderie of the Trek it wasn't.

There were three Canadians on the Trek - Fred from Winnipeg, Manitoba, Johnny Van Tol from Vancouver, British Columbia and myself from Victoria (ferry ride across the Juan de Fuca strait to Vancouver and Seattle.) I didn't know Fred that well. His work prevented him from starting the Trek in June, so he joined us at the half way point, having like a true Manitoban completed the first half on his own during the winter months.

Chapter 6

Day 28 Wabasha Minnesota to Sparta Wisconsin 91 miles as remembered by Trekkers Guy Smith #280, Mary Fleming #27, Nancy Easel #6, Sharon White #291, Woody Wood #237, Karin Allen #29 and Marianne Brems #49

(Guy Smith #280) Next morning very early I started alone, hoping to get ahead of the muggy heat that was sure to return. In the first mile we crossed the Mississippi for the last time and entered the Badger State, Wisconsin.

Early morning pictures documented this event, and I joined up with 'Team Out Of Control" in a fast pace line, a great way to make some progress before the heat became to intense. That morning another landmark was reached - 2000 miles! As we celebrated and took pictures, we started to realize the extent of our accomplishment. Crossing the US by bicycle was beginning to feel like a reality. Later, because of the heat, we slowed way down and welcomed every opportunity to rest, especially when we were invited to pick and eat strawberries for free. In the afternoon I rode with Cam and Ellen from Alaska. We had lunch at a restaurant along the Mississippi River and then bid farewell to the "Big Muddy" as we took the first of the Wisconsin bike trails. This state is a pacesetter in the nationwide 'Rails to Trails" program, where old railroad beds are converted to bike trails. The trails are not paved but are made with fairly fine crushed gravel which becomes

a very smooth biking surface when it gets packed down. The trails provide many advantages to long distance bicyclists. A reprieve from traffic, noise, and fumes, gradual grades because trains cannot climb steep inclines and forested trails which are shady and cool. After 20 miles on the trail we reluctantly returned to the county roads. Nobody wanted to believe that we actually had to climb a road paved straight up the side of a mile high hill. It was dubbed "Killer Hill" and was voted as the steepest climb of the entire Trek - even steeper than roads in the Rockies or the Appalachians ahead of us. We decided to have a second lunch, a picnic in the park at West Salem. There a toddler named Ben was so thrilled playing with the horn on my bike that his mom couldn't drag him away. He was celebrating his First Birthday so I gave him one of my Colorado pins as a souvenir. With 95 miles under our belt for the day, we dragged ourselves into camp on the Sparta High School football field and shared in the grand welcome for Olga, a Sparta native.

(Woody Wood #237) Woody said "You never knew from day to day who you were going to meet and what their story might be. This evening John Riley and I were in a bar. We were sitting next to a very talkative man who tells us he was just paroled from prison where he served his time for murder."

Wisconsin

(Mary Fleming #27) Breakfast was at the local church and was served by a group that was going to follow up with a fund raising pancake breakfast. That seemed like a good idea to me and avoided the possibility of lots of left over's that might go to waste.

We crossed to the east side of the river this morning to Wisconsin and rode through some river delta areas. There was lots of water and marsh land and we went for quite a way without seeing much of the real river. The river is much more impressive as we go further south on it. There is a lot of boat activity, both commercial and recreational. I stopped for awhile and watched the lock activity. There are some really long barge trains on the river. The one I watched would not all fit in the lock so they moved the front end in and moored it and then pulled the back half out while the front end was dropped to the lower level. Then they somehow moved the front half of the train out of the lock, But I could not determine how it was being powered They then brought the second half in and took it through.

The weather is just miserable. Still very hot and muggy. The effort of riding seems extreme but the breeze created by riding helps keep a little cooler than when you just stand still. The countryside is very pretty with lots of farms growing primarily corn and wheat, it seems. Today we hit the 2,000 mile mark.

(Marianne Brems #49) I've never known a time when I've enjoyed a swim so much plus it's an environment I know. I can hardly remember the last time I swam because of heat.

(Nancy Eiselt #6) I rode the entire day today with Karin Van der Velden. We really took our time, talked a lot and stopped a lot. Our first stop out of Wabasha was in Cochrane, where we indulged in Sunday breakfast, complete with Sunday paper. Because the café wasn't directly on the route, it wasn't a "Trekker Trap", and we were "the most exciting thing to happen to the place in years," as one other customer put it.

(Sharon White #291) Knowing that I would be in the United States for Canada Day, I asked the Canadian Government to send me Canadian flags and pins. They arrived at a mail stop. I had enough pins to go around, but only 100 flags, so Johnny and I celebrated Canada Day with a Canadian-style Jeopardy game. At dinner, we set out to give out as many Canadian flags as we could. Recipients would be successful by answering skill testing questions about Canada. Questions like - who's our Prime Minister? It was Brian Mulroney, but everyone answered Pierre Trudeau. No one could correctly answer the question about which province has a half hour time zone. It's Newfoundland, but in fairness, most Canadians can't answer that correctly either. Frank, from Philadelphia staunchly refused to believe this time and a space anomaly even when we explained that Newfoundland is kind of like a Canadian New Jersey - it get's no respect and is subject to "Nufy" jokes. So a half hour is pretty much par for the course when it comes to Canada's easternmost province. My favorite attempt at getting a flag though, was Jeff Green's rendition of our national anthem, O Canada, sung to the tune of "Oh Christmas Tree" Priceless and flag-worthy. The next day I felt a special pride as my fellow Trekkers rode by, resplendent with a small Canadian flag posted on their handlebars. And that's how spending your national holiday in another country amongst more that 300 new American friends, becomes that much less lonely.

(Karin Allen # 29) It's impossible to imagine, but the WORST HILL on the entire Trek was in Wisconsin! Worse than the Cascades, Rockies, or headwinds. I couldn't believe it, but after riding 2000 miles, I found myself getting off and pushing my bike up the hill! The good news was at the top, "Dr Jeff" was waiting with a big block of ice that we happily got to have perched on our backs for a few minutes to help cool us off.

Day 29 Sparta Wisconsin to Baraboo Wisconsin 82 miles as remembered by Trekkers Mike Mitchell #1, Guy Smith #280, Mary Fleming #27, Nancy Eiselt #6 and Marianne Brems #49

(Mike Mitchell #1) What a beautiful day and the tunnels were fun but I had my eyes set on getting to town in time to go to the Barnum and Bailey Museum and see a circus performance. Arrived in camp before 2:00 p.m. I had plenty of time to rest and get ready for the circus. Gathered about five or six other Trekkers and we all had a great evening. I have always loved the big top and when I was a kid in Riverside, California the circus parade would go by our house and the elephants would pick pomegranates off our corner tree and the circus people would give Mom and Dad free passes for all of us. Sometimes we would go down and help feed the animals.Slept good that night dreaming of clowns and trapeze artists.

(Guy Smith # 280) Breakfast this morning was at a restaurant belonging to Olga's family, and I was invited to share it with all of them who gathered there to send off their favorite Trekker. This was one of the most enjoyable days of the Trek, starting with the first 35 miles along the Sparta-Elroy bicycle trail, one of the most famous trails in all of North America. The trail winds through beautiful forests and tunnels cross the steepest hills. These are very dark tunnels, one being a mile long, so we couldn't ride our bikes inside them, though some tried and became completely disoriented in the darkness even with flashlights. I rode with Fred and Johnnie both from Canada who were both superb riders. On the smooth crushed gravel we maintained a sporting pace over 20 mph. Back on the country roads again, I rode by myself for the rest of morning enjoying the steep hills and the picturesque farmlands. Of all the states, Wisconsin was best at providing interesting pastoral scenery mile after mile. At Reedsburg I had lunch with Damian from Great Britain. By now he had become a great fan of the American milk shake, something they don't have in England and he ranted about there goodness in his cockney accent to the delight of those who served him. We rode together to Baraboo, the home of the Barnum & Bailey Circus, and our home for the evening. We camped that night on the grounds of the Wisconsin National Guard Armory. Despite the heat I had a busy evening of laundry, bike cleaning and writing post cards.

(Marianne Brems #49) Heat is still the dominant theme. The character of the Trek has changed. Energy is lower. The West Coast people are suffering. Only the Floridians and the Southerners are thriving. Even my writing is slowing down. We need another Garrison Keillor story again tonight.

(Mary Fleming #27) Today the ride was over 30 miles on the Elroy-Sparta State Trail which follows the old railway route. There are 3 tunnels and many bridges. We need much more of this type of facility in this country. It is really great to be able to ride off the roads and not have to compete with automobile and truck traffic. There was a lot of traffic out today as people took off for the holiday a little early.

The one drawback to the trail is that it is fairly level with very little up and down and therefore little chance to rest on the bike.

My lower back was causing a lot of pain after about half the day so I got a ride into the Wisconsin National Guard Armory at Baraboo. It was very hot (Low 90's) but a little less humid than yesterday.

(Nancy Eiselt #6)I've really enjoyed my last two days on the road, in spite of the heat and humidity. The temperature's been well into the 90's and it's been really sticky - but not as sticky as I expect to be as we continue eastward. It makes for hazy days, challenging cycling and perpetually damp skin. I'm guzzling water and juice just to keep up with the water I perspire out.

Day 30 Baraboo Wisconsin to Lake Mills WI 69 miles as remembered by Trekkers Guy Smith #280, Mary Fleming #27, Nancy Eiselt #6 and Marianne Brems #49

(Marianne Brems #49) I don't really remember a lot about this day except it was hot and humid like nearly all of our days in the Midwest. So it was inviting to think of taking a dip. Also, it is in my nature when faced with any body of water to think, first, how can I get in it? And second, does it make sense to get in it? Please note the order of these two questions which is significant. I think of practicality when it comes to swimming. My Mother tells me that I started this when I was very young, in fact before I could walk. She likes to tell the story about when I was one year and a few months old. We lived by the North Sea in Denmark and she would walk me in my stroller. She says if I was in the stroller I was fine, but if for any reason I wasn't restricted, I'd head for the water. She found this out one day when we were out and she stopped to talk to a friend after lifting me out of the stroller. Before she knew it I had taken off on all fours and continued straight into the water, clothes and all.

Anyway, back to Wisconsin. I think another contributing factor that day was that we all were in the mode of "get there under your own steam" and I just felt like, why should I stop just because there is a river to cross? Who needs a ferry? And I had friends willing to take my bike on the ferry for me and there was a hose on the other side to hose the green slime out of my shorts and sports bra. It all made perfect sense to me especially since there weren't any signs saying no swimming.

(**Guy Smith #280**) Tuesday was the fourth of July and Michelle and I had volunteered to sweep. That meant we would get a very late start and would have a long day trying to stay at the tail end of all the Trekkers. I wanted to start the day by sleeping in, but my body was to accustomed to early rising. While we waited for the late starters to talk themselves into getting on the road, Michelle decorated our bikes for the holiday with red, white and blue balloons and streamers. It was already intensely hot when we finally got on the road at 9:30, and we welcomed the shady highway along Devil's Lake that took us to the Ferry across the Wisconsin river. Marianne from California, not to be cheated out of this precious quarter mile across the river, swam alongside the ferry while her bike rode across. We had a difficult time staying behind slower riders so we spent a lot of time sharing in the 4th of July festivities at Lodi, the home of Susie the duck. Each year Susie hatches her young in a concrete planter along the main street and the site is duly marked with a large sign. We had an ice cream snack in Waunakee which claims to be "the only Waunakee in the World". This area is one of the prettiest we've seen; from the top of any hill you can see hundreds of silos and small neat farms with bright red barns and farmhouses. The farms gave way to the lively city of Madison, state capital and home of the University of Wisconsin. We rode into town along the shores of Lake Mendota; shared in some of the holiday festivities and visited the state capital building, a beautiful four winged structure capped with a huge dome. Sweeping in a large city is almost impossible so we gave up around 5:30 leaving the rest of the job to the sweep vehicle which remained behind to encourage any stragglers. Routinely I arrived in camp by mid-afternoon, so on that day I enjoyed the early evening ride,It was cooler and the sun at our backs cast long shadows along the rural roads. The sun was setting as we rode along Rock Lake into the town of Lake Mills. Fireworks and a street dance were on tap for the evening, but I had only enough energy to put up my tent, eat, shower and go to bed. Our day as "Team Sweep" was much more difficult than my previous one with Wendy going to Malta, Montana.

(Mary Fleming #27) I left Baraboo very early, again trying for the cool part of the day. I knew, from the minute I got on the bike that I wouldn't ride for long. My back is still hurting badly after riding a few miles. We went through Devil's lake state park and then down to Merrimac on the Wisconsin river.We got across the river on the ferry. That was about 13 miles into the day. I then got a ride into Madison and wandered around town a bit on my bike. I went to see Frank Lloyd Wright's "Unitarian Church". The strong triangular forms create a really strong statement.

When I finished exploring, I got a ride the rest of the way into Lake Mills where I found someone that was driving into Milwaukee and was willing to give me a lift. I left my bike with the Trek and headed for town. Since Milwaukee was a rest day, I thought that two days of rest and a real bed for three nights would help my back recover.

(Nancy Eiselt #6) Team Monopod reconvened today. We "putzed" much of the day, but also moved at a fair pace in the afternoon. Our first stop was only five miles into the ride, after several hill climbs and one of the best downhill runs we've had yet. It was s-curve after s-curve, shady and cool; what a blast. We got to Devil's Lake and stopped for Janice to swim. Beautiful lake, and only a few boats were on it. We had the shore to ourselves. Janice plunged right in, while the rest of us ventured in up to our short lines. The water was clear and surprisingly warm. After a half hour lounging break we wandered out of the park via the restrooms and that was when we saw the warning posted about "swimmers itch". Evidently, the lake is full of these worms that penetrate the skin and cause itching, redness and swelling and leave evidence of their presence by causing red welts. We all had a good laugh about it, particularly Janice, because she was riding in her wet biking shorts. Who knows how many critters were crawling around in there.

Day 31 Lake Mills WI to Milwaukee WI 54 miles as remembered by Trekkers Guy Smith #280, Mike Mitchell #1, Karin Allen # 29, Ellen Lowe #42 and Marianne Brems #49

(Guy Smith #280) This morning I rode with Karin, and we began with 26 delightful miles along the Glacial Drumlin Trail. Back on the highway we were enjoying the ups and downs of the short hills when suddenly Karin's rear wheel skidded on some gravel and she went down. I was directly behind her and as she fell on the right shoulder of the road her bike landed directly in front of mine. I rolled over her bike and came crashing down almost on top of her. Her bicycle and my left elbow suffered the worst damage. We were both badly shaken up when Peter from Massachusetts came along to help. He had a first aid kit and cleaned my arm, removed a very large pebble that made me grimace in pain and bandaged me up. He did such a good job that I was able to ride to the checkpoint at Wales where Lloyd our Paramedic, finished up the job. Luckily Karin suffered only scratches and was able to ride her crumpled bike after some minor road repairs. We had to sooth the pain with an extra large Dairy Queen Blizzard -- Karin's treat. Soon the beautiful Wisconsin farms turned into suburbs and then into big city. We crossed through the grounds of the huge VA Medical Center, past the sprawling Miller Brewery into the bustling city center.

(Mike Mitchell #1) Started the day riding with most of Team Geritol. One of our favorite things is to sing old songs and get ten or fifteen miles under our belts. Things sort of fell apart when we hit the Glacial Drumlin Trail. It is in amazing shape and easy to ride on. Am really working on keeping my cadence high and protecting the knees. Also trying to remember to get off and stretch after the first ten miles. Knock on wood I still haven't had a single flat tire on the ride. Try to be careful and have walked my bike a few times on bad spots where others rode.

(Karin Allen #29) My only real accident of the Trek occurred when I hit some gravel while riding with Guy. My bike went down and he was able to stop and did a rolling flip over me. My bike got pretty bent up and I scraped my elbow. Guy had it worse, however, as he actually had a rock imbedded in his elbow (ick) Once we were all patched up I was able to get my bike working again, we had Blizzards (as usual) to help ease the pain.

(Ellen Lowe #42) I remember "Team Denim", Jim and Kathy Koepp who rode every single mile of every single day in blue jeans. Jim swore he never had a pair of cycling shorts on in his life and he never would. He also carried a huge tool box like the kind a mechanic carries; it must have weighed 15 to 20 pounds. Boy was he prepared to fix anything.

(Marianne Brems #49) Looking at Lake Michigan is like looking at the ocean. There's a red thing on top of the gas building that looks either like a flame or like a grenade. Apparently it changes color according to what the weather is going to be.Blue for cold, red for hot, etc. When you ask people about it everyone has a different answers. Some people haven't even noticed it.

Day 32 Milwaukee Wisconsin rest day 0 miles as remembered by Trekkers Guy Smith #280, Nancy Eiselt #6, Kevin Collins #25, Joe Siebold #48 and Marianne Brems #49

BIO JOE SIEBOLD #48

The reason I did the 1989 Trek was because I stopped smoking, which was one of the hardest things I did in my life. I also wanted to raise money for the American Lung Association for research.

(Joe Siebold #48) This was the favorite day of the trip for me. Since I live only 80 miles north of Milwaukee I was able to spend the night at home celebrating my son's ninth birthday.

(Guy Smith #280) We stayed in the dorms of the downtown campus of Marquette University, a catholic college famous for it's outstanding basketball program. Milwaukee was celebrating "Summerfest" a gala festival along the waterfront of Lake Michigan consisting mainly of carnival rides and musical concerts. Sightseeing and shopping were on everybody's agenda plus good restaurants movies and relaxing. I was grateful for the rest day to give my left elbow a chance to heal.

(Nancy Eiselt #6) I think people are beginning to realize that we have a very short time left before we will be parting ways and returning to our "former" lives. Lots of people are taking more time on the road, socializing more, and really trying to smell the roses. I often feel that I'm with the same people a lot. But I enjoy them and am trying now to spend quality time. I've enjoyed rooming with Janice and riding with "Team Monopod", I hope I'll keep in touch with them after Trek is but a memory.

(Marianne Brems #49) A theme that is emerging is a feeling of not wanting to have anyone come and visit you on Trek, perhaps so the bubble won't burst. Others are experiencing it to.

BIO KEVIN COLLINS #25

In 1989 I was just starting my career with Edison Mission Energy. Just before the ride I was a temp with them. I had shown enough to have them offer me a permanent job, but I told them I couldn't since I would be doing the Transamerica Trek. The controller was impressed with the fact I didn't take the job and then quit at the time of the ride. With this she said I could still have the job and do the ride. And the company donated $1,000. It was good to come back to a job. I was living in Fountain Valley, California at the time.

(Kevin Collins #25) Tom Brucker, Gina Mix and I rode to Chicago today and spent the night at the house of Wendy Williams (staff) mom. I had to get to Chicago early since I had set up the day at the baseball game (Cubs versus Dodgers) for about 60 Trekkers and I had to put the tickets in the individual envelopes at Wrigley Field. The three of us left Milwaukee without the use of a trip tik. We just figured we had to go south and keep the lake on our left side. Initially we had trouble when we rode into an industrial area just outside of Milwaukee and kept finding dead end streets. The day was a test on the tires. That night we relaxed and had dinner at Gino's on Rush Street.

Chapter 7

Day 33 Milwaukee WI to Chicago IL 89 miles as remembered by Trekkers Guy Smith #280, Andy Rasutis #269, Karin Allen #29 and Marianne Brems #49

NOTE: *Trekker William Sutherland # 137 was presented in the Chicago Police Star, the official publication of the Chicago Police Department, as a Transamerica Trekker. William said "He felt it important for the public to know the Chicago Police Department is aware and concerned about charitable organizations such as the American Lung Association, and that officer's care".*

BIO ANDY RASUTIS #269

In 1989 I was 2 years out of college (25 years old). I was working for a HVAC contractor who went bankrupt. I was playing hockey with a local team and just started dating my wife, Alice. I knew that it was time to get serious with my career and my life. I decided to do this Trek before time-constraints and obligations would dictate otherwise. I always dreamed of riding across America. It never seemed possible until now. I would love to ride the same course with my kids, when they are older.

(**Andy Rasutis #269**) My best experiences were numerous. Climbing the mountain on the first day.Coming down a mountain road at 51 mph. Meeting all the wonderful people on Trek and the hundreds of people who came out to meet...greet... and feed us every night. Riding through my hometown (Chicago) and spending the night with my family. I met and rode with a group of great people. We were the "Beyond Hope" team which inclued, Wendy Armstrong, Alison Parker, John, Sharon Perry, and Rick Heath.

(**Marianne Brems #49**) On the trip through Lake Forest all

Sunrise 47

you could hear were blowers and weed eaters. Gayle Delanty hugged me and we talked about de-trekking. She was a stitch when she talked about buying jeans at Kmart. They kept calling it "your Kmart" she said. I've never seen so many McDonalds.

(Guy Smith #280) Friday was a day with a purpose. We had tickets to the Cubs-Dodgers game which was being played in Chicago at 12:30 a.m., 87 miles away. Before dawn seven of us were pedaling our way through the empty streets of Milwaukee, determined to be in Chicago before the game started. We decided not to follow the suggested route on the trip tik but instead took U.S. 32 and Sheridan road along the lake front, the shortest way we could find between Milwaukee and Chicago. With 5 miles under our belt, our bodies cried out for breakfast. We found an open café, but the meal didn't slow us down for long, soon we were speeding along again in a pace line through the busy Wisconsin towns, mixing in with the morning rush hour traffic of Racine and Kenosha. We stopped very quickly for pictures at the Illinois border and at the US Naval station at Great Lakes my first Navy home. In Illinois, Sheridan Road winds through millionaire communities like Lake Forest and Winnetka but we hardly saw the sights as we kept pounding as fast as our legs would let us. At 10:30 a.m. we came to a stop in front of Mertz Hall on the campus of Loyola University in Chicago. Feeling proud and victorious, we ignored screaming muscles and aching bones and made plans to shower and afterwards to meet and go to the ball game together. Historic Wrigley Field and the exciting Chicago Cubs made the "Pace Line From Hell" worth the effort. The sellout crowd cheered the Cubs to a 6-4 victory over the Los Angeles Dodgers. Later we took the subway downtown and enjoyed a spectacular view of the city from atop the Hancock Building. In another part of town, Terri Sears and some other Trekkers were enjoying a tour of the city with Jeff Green an architect from Dallas. Jeff marveled at the architectural wonders of this huge city, shared his knowledge about buildings with his friends and enjoyed a relaxing evening on the town. Jeff's friends remembered his delight; they could see that he truly enjoyed visiting Chicago and admired the architects who designed the huge skyscrapers around him. Our group returned to Loyola by subway in time to share in a pizza party hosted by the Chicago Chapter of the American Lung Association. My stamina didn't last very long; I preferred to retire to the 18th floor of the college dorm. There my room was filled with a delightful breeze wafting off the lake which sent me quickly to dreamland.

(**Karin Allen #29**) Chicago! It was a beautiful day as I rode along the shores of Lake Michigan with Terri, Nancy and Guy. We had a good time with Guy taking pictures on the beach, playing up to our nickname of the "Nordy Girls." We continued our ride along the lake near Shedd Aquarium when I heard a noise behind me and saw Terri flip over the front of her bike and land on her face. I screamed for Guy and Nancy, who got back immediately. Terri was bleeding badly, but luckily was conscious. She had broken a tooth and had skinned herself up badly on her face, chin and chest. Before I knew it, Ingrid, who thankfully was a nurse, was there handling the situation, and very soon police and ambulance arrived on the scene. It was such a helpless feeling to stand there as she was driving away to the hospital, as we didn't know really how badly she was injured or when we would see her again. After looking at her bike, we discovered that somehow her front fender had caught on her wheel and folded up, which jammed her wheel and threw her forward. What a freak accident. It was bad enough to have to negotiate our way through the south side of Chicago, but to do so with the thoughts of Terri in our heads made it all the harder. We were glad to ride over the border to Indiana and leave Illinois behind us.

Day 34 Chicago Illinois to Valparaiso Indiana 78 miles as remembered by Trekkers Guy Smith #280, Mary Fleming #27, Nancy Eiselt #6, Roger Whidden #190 and Marianne Brems #49

(**Guy Smith #280**) Nobody was excited about our Saturday ride, one that required a three page trip tik to guide us through South Chicago streets, heavily industrialized neighborhoods, and the crowded highways of North Indiana. However, the first 15 miles was on the busy but delightful Lakeshore Bikeway which parallels the beaches of Lake Michigan. I rode with the "Nordy Girls" Karin, Nancy and Terri. They loved to pose for pictures like the cutesy models of the classy Nordstrom's Department Stores; we got several good ones that morning. I was leading our group. Terri, normally a very intense rider, was lagging way behind. As we were passing Shedd Aquarium, Karin suddenly yelled. "Terri is down." In her mirror Karin had seen her friend flying headfirst over the handlebars and landing on her head in the bike bath. I rushed back to Terri where she lay with a large pool of blood beginning to form around her mouth and face. A passing jogger offered to run to a street telephone to get help. Teri was conscious but bleeding badly. Her tooth was broken. Both lips and her face were skinned, and she had many bruises on her shoulders and chest. She was a very beautiful woman with a big warm smile and I felt so helpless to see her lying there. The only thing I could do was direct traffic, keeping bicycles and joggers clear of her so that nothing worse would happen. Nobody dared moved her before the ambulance arrived. Ingrid, a nurse Trekker rode up and took over the first aid. Terri asked me 'What did I do wrong?" I didn't know but when I examined her bike, I found out that she had a fender that jammed into the tire and had crumpled up into the brake. When the wheel suddenly locked without warning, her body continued its momentum and she went sailing over the handlebars. Because of her helmet she had no head injuries. Within 15 minutes police and an ambulance arrived and took her, accompanied by Ingrid to a hospital. It took another half hour to contact somebody from the Trek staff to come and pick up the two bikes. As we waited, the three of us hugged and cried together feeling very disheartened by the accident to our friend. I was convinced that this was the worst thing that could happen on this trip. It was awful! All day long we talked about Terri. Everyone had heard about the accident and kept asking us what happened.

    Fortunately the staff kept in touch with the hospital, and we were updated regularly about her progress along the road. The Trek had a wonderful ham radio network to communicate with all the rode vehicles and the two base camps connected by volunteer radio operators along the route. First we found out that Terri had broken a tooth and needed stitches inside her mouth, but she had been treated and released to go to an emergency dental clinic. Later we learned that she was in great pain but was going to Valparaiso, Indiana and would stay in a hotel there for the night. Meanwhile Karin, Nancy and I made our way through South Chicago, "The baddest part of town". On every street corner we were sure we would come face to face with "Big Bad Leroy Brown, the Baddest Man in the whole damn town". Nancy picked this wonderful location to have her first flat tire of the Trek. We circled around her in the middle of an empty lot, and I was elected to fend off any "attackers" while Nancy changed the tire. Nobody bothered us and we were soon on the road again. I give credit to the Trekker staff who scouted out that route. I know the area very well, and there isn't a good way to go thru South Chicago and Northern Indiana; but our route wasn't to bad and even had some delightful spots that surprised us. When we entered Indiana, our 8th state; the Saturday afternoon traffic was frightful along U.S. Route 30, one of the busiest four-lane highways in the country. A local cyclist named Bruce joined us and pointed out some of the sites; nobody was interested. We all just wanted to get out of the heat and away from the incessant traffic. Nancy wanted to get to Valparaiso fast to see her husband's family. When we arrived, her whole gang ambushed her and belted her with water balloons. I joined in the fun because it was cool. After showers we found a Dairy Queen, had blizzards, and bought cards to send to Terri at the hotel. She didn't want any visitors. We were staying in the dorms of the Valparaiso University and when I returned there, I was surprised by another family visit; all of Joe's family - Donna, Adam, Heidi, Ann-Marie, Tom, Beth, Josh and Amy. I felt like a celebrity. They took me home to Tom and Ann-Marie's house for dinner and a pleasant evening with the family. Their home was about 20 miles from the campus and we drove along SR49 which would be our route next morning. I was relieved to hear Tom say that there would be almost no traffic on that road early Sunday morning, except for a few people getting off the night shift at the nearby mill. We had our fill of traffic that day and I looked foreword to a carefree day in rural, flat Indiana. I noticed that SR 49 had no shoulders. That night I slept fretfully with memories of Terri's accident vividly dancing around my subconscious. It was a brutally hot evening with no breeze, and most people slept uncovered with their doors open. About 3:00 a.m. a weak frontal system passed through the area with rain and wind, causing doors to slam shut along the corridor. I couldn't get back to sleep, so I decided to get up around 5:00 a.m.

(**Mary Fleming #27**) We are staying at Valparaiso University. So far I have no roommate, but it is only 9 p.m. and people are still coming in. I didn't get in until 7 p.m. We started at 6:30 a.m. in a small group, as recommended throughout Chicago. But after 16 miles I spotted the Chicago Museum of Science and Industry which had a Frank Lloyd Wright exhibit. I actually only noticed the exhibit because Nancy brought it to my attention knowing that I was interested. I decided to pull out of the group, after getting assurances from the van that they would be there for at least a couple of hours. Jim then decided to go with me. We ended up spending three and a half hours there and had lunch and saw the bicycle exhibit. It looks like a really interesting and stimulating museum and I wished that we had more time. Apparently some people stayed until 4 p.m. and are just now straggling in. Not too considerate of staff, who have to stay on duty until everyone is accounted for.

This place has fireflies with bright chartreuse lights. They are really great. The ride took us along the waterfront for 16 miles and then through a low income, high traffic area of Chicago and then into some nice middle income, low traffic area. The difference in roadway quality was impressive. We then went through a strip commercial area. Generally up until the last 17 miles the roads were miserable.

It was very hot today, up into the 90's. One person said his thermometer read 100 (mine never went above 90) It was in the mid 90's I WOULD GUESS. We are only 15 miles from the lake, but you would never guess it.

I will try to start early tomorrow and there probably won't be much reason to stop. We are generally headed south toward Indianapolis. We entered our 8th state today - Indiana.

(**Nancy Eiselt#6**) What a day!A stressful one but also a very fun one, by day's end. I'd made plans to get an early start so I could meet the Billey clan (my in-laws) in Valparaiso by 1:00 p.m. Breakfast was light and relatively quick, and by 6:15 a.m. Guy Smith, Karin Van Der Velden, Terri Sears and I were on the road. I think we were all a bit apprehensive about the ride through the south side of Chicago, but we were enjoying the ride along Lakeshore Drive. Terri started lagging behind a little, which I thought very uncharacteristic of her. I kept looking back for her, and she seemed fine. I'll never forget, though, when Karin screamed, just ten miles into the ride, "Terri went down!"

We wheeled around to check on her, and she was lying still on the pavement, a small pool of blood forming on the sidewalk by her mouth. She looked conscious but wasn't moving. I felt so helpless, my first aid kit was useless, and I didn't want to move her. Fortunately a bystander phoned for an ambulance, which arrived within ten minutes. I knew Terri was OK, though, when she asked me to take a picture of her! She looked so bad, bloody, swollen, smashed tooth. I'm sure now that the bruises have set in it looks even more spectacular. I got a really eerie feeling when she told me she'd dreamt this would happen all along...

I kept thinking about Terri all day, as I'm sure Karin and Guy did. It made us all realize just how great the potential for injurious accidents is on a trip like this, even for the strong and cautious riders like Terri. With less than two weeks to go, it'll be easy for people to start being careless, getting over tired, and having accidents. God, I hope I'm not one of the casualties.

(Roger Whidden #190) Met Jeff Green at dinner outside Indy I'm going on and on about how amazing it is how no one has died on this Trek or the previous two Treks. 12 hours later Jeff is dead.

(Marianne Brems #49) Swimming in Lake Michigan at 7:30 a.m. in the morning was a delight. I hadn't planned to do it, but there it was. Everyone was ruffled by the heat, the traffic and the bumps today. Perhaps the urban environment is upsetting our delicate sensibilities which are not used to the pressure of urban living.

Day 35 Valparaiso Indiana to Delphi Indiana 80 miles as remembered by Trekkers Guy Smith #280, Mike Mitchell #1,

Sunrise 47

Mary Fleming #27, Laura Remaly #185, Nancy Eiselt #6, Sharon White #291, Hubert "Woody" Wood #237, Nancy Ackles #124, Karin Allen #29 and Marianne Brems #49

(Guy Smith #280) At breakfast I ran into Karin who wanted to ride with me today. I was glad to see that she wasn't spooked because we had experienced troubles the last two times we rode together; first our own spill on the way to Milwaukee and then witnessing Terri's accident just the day before. It was drizzling lightly when we got on the road, but already it was warming up, promising to be a humid scorcher. As we turned off the main road onto highway 49, we were talking about how lethargic we felt, like everything was in slow motion. It was around 6:30 a.m.. Up ahead we saw a commotion in the road, several bikes were laying in the roadway and somebody was on the ground. Karin screamed, "Oh God, No Not Again". At first I thought somebody was just taking some goofy pictures as Trekkers often did. But as we got closer, I could see at least one bike was terribly wrecked with the wheel completely smashed. I couldn't figure out how two bikers going the same direction could collide and cause that much damage. Jerry Wright from Seattle, was sitting on the side of the road holding his leg. He was yelling to me to chase down a yellow car that had hit him and then left the scene. Then I saw Jeff Green. I had a sickening flashback to the day before; Jeff was lying in a pool of blood. Bruce who had been riding ahead of Jeff and Jerry had returned to help out and was performing CPR on Jeff. I had an awful sinking feeling in my stomach. Karin was just standing there, her mouth open, with a look of horror on her face. Slowly the terrible truth began to sink in - Jeff was not breathing. A car came by, and we asked him to call an ambulance and the police. Another car came by with two nurses on their way to work, they immediately started working on Jeff. Karin and I felt so helpless. Neither one of us knew CPR. Again there was nothing I could do but direct traffic. Other bicyclists and cars started arriving. Soon the place was covered with police, ambulances and fire trucks, volunteer fire department cars and Trek staff vehicles. We just stood there shaking, crying and holding each other. As cyclists arrived, they were encouraged to keep going. Some did, others stayed and stared in disbelief as the two injured men were taken away in ambulances. Some of the cyclists were rerouted from the campus to another road, so many knew nothing of the accident. I wanted to go to the church and pray for Jeff; Karin wanted to go home. Most people sat alongside that road holding on to each other and saying nothing. I said "It's only a bike ride. It's suppose to be fun It's not suppose to be like this." Nobody dared to say the word "death", fearing that saying it might make it happen. I got on my bike and left the others deciding to ride to Tom and Ann-Mare's house so they could give me a ride to church. On my way I crossed a road where some other bicyclists were riding. Cam, Ellen and Janna came along having a happy chat as they rode. As soon as they saw me they knew something was wrong, and I had to tell them about Jeff and Jerry. They decided to ride with me. Even though it would take them about 8 miles out of the way. As we rode, Ellen tried to get me to slow down; I was pumping a huge amount of adrenaline. She rode alongside me and spontaneously began to pray out loud. There in the midst of all of this tragedy, I felt the warmth of bonding with a fellow Trekker. Something told me that it would take an awful lot of bonding for us to survive this morning's tragedy. At Tom and Ann-Marie's we woke up the household, and within minutes Donna was ready to drive me wherever I wanted to go. We retraced my route to the scene of the accident but nobody was there. It was so weird - there wasn't a trace, as if I had dreamed the whole thing. Next we went back to Valparaiso University and found Karin and about 7 others who were sitting on the lawn waiting for some word from the hospital. Nobody wanted to go anywhere, so Donna took me to a nearby church. I prayed for Jeff to live, but an overwhelming feeling came over me that he would not. When we came out I told Donna "Jeff is dead". Arriving back at the University, Karin gave us the official word; Jeff was dead on arrival at the hospital; Jerry had a broken leg and would be released soon. There was still no word on the hit-and-run driver. But there was a search going on for him or her. The only clues were yellow paint on the wrecked bicycles and an automobile antenna broken off in the collision. Karin wanted to go to church so we loaded her bike in Donna's car and went with her. The others decided to start riding - there was nothing else to do. Donna drove me and Karin to Tom and Ann-Marie's house where we had something to eat and made some phone calls. Karin was a wreck and wanted to fly home, but her boyfriend and family in Seattle convinced her to try to ride on. I called my Mom and cried on the phone as I told her the story. It was almost 1:00 p.m. Karin and I decided to ask Donna to drive us to the med-day check point at Francesville, and we would start biking there. Checkpoint, normally lively and chaotic, was a very sad experience. As each bicyclist arrived, someone from the volunteer staff hugged then and told them what had happened. It was a very sensitive and caring way to break the news. Some just sat there in disbelief; some went to a nearby church to pray and be comforted; others just got back on their bikes and started riding, mostly alone. The staff had their hands full dealing with the tragedy back in Valparaiso trying to keep the bike Trek on track, dealing with those who were overwhelmed, and trying to set up for the night in Delphi. Karin and I hadn't been riding too long when, suddenly my rear wheel started wobbling badly. We stopped several times and I tried to tighten it but couldn't find the problem. Then Don from Hawaii came along and told me that my frame was broken. I was devastated. I couldn't ride anymore that day, so the others went on, and I waited for a sag wagon to come along. When it came I got in - the toughest thing I had to do on the Trek. Jerry was in the van sitting lengthwise on the seat. His left leg in a knee-length cast. For a long time I didn't know what to say to him and just held his hand. Finally I asked him "how do you feel Jerry?" He answered "The trouble is I feel to damn good". I thought about what he said; he meant that he should be dead instead of Jeff Then I said "No Jerry, the trouble is that Jeff is dead. You shouldn't be dead. You deserve to be alive. The trouble is that Jeff deserves to be alive to. But he's dead". We didn't say much more as we drove past frightened bicyclists along the road. The heat and humidity were unbearable and the Sunday drivers, returning from a weekend at Schaefer Lake, harassed and heckled the bicyclists, unaware of the heavy burden they carried. It was a somber troop that arrived at the Delphi High School that evening. Most decided to stay indoors, because the school was air conditioned. Terri arrived by car from the hotel in Valparaiso in time for supper. Her pretty face was covered with bandages and Neosporin. She wanted to sit with me in a quiet corner where nobody had to look at her while they ate. But all of her friends flocked around her telling her how glad we were that she was alive. That evening we gathered in the school auditorium where the staff leaders, Dave and Gayle, told the story of the accident. Some people stood up and told stories about Jeff.

Especially those who really knew him well. A picture was passed around so that those who didn't know him could see who he was. A suggestion was made to take up a collection for a remembrance at his funeral and another collection to offer a reward to find the hit and run driver. We decided to wear green ribbons on our bikes to carry with us the spirit of Jeff Green. Roi a Trekker from the Virgin Islands ended the meeting with a song he made up on the road.

We learned the chorus and sang it with him, first timidly and then with gusto. Long into the night, small bands of people stayed awake talking and comforting each other. Everyone wondered if it was possible to recover from this and to arrive in Atlantic City with the enthusiasm and fun we had anticipated. The healing process was already beginning.

(Mike Mitchell #1) Initially this was just another day. As usual I was one of the first Trekkers out of camp. Hoped to pick up some other riders down the road and try to form a pace line if I could find a group that rode in my speed range. As it turned out I never met up with anyone and before I knew it I was coming into the mid-day checkpoint. I was kind of surprised that there wasn't anyone hollering or making noise. I started to get a feeling in my stomach that something was wrong when I looked around and saw that everyone looked sad and a couple of Trekker's were crying. I don't remember who came up to me and took me aside but they were very concerned on how I would react when I was told about Jeff. All I remember is thanking whoever told me. They said I could keep riding or if I wanted to they were bringing in buses to take Trekkers to the next camp if I didn't feel like riding. I said I definitely wanted to keep riding and off I went. The remainder of the day was sort of a fog thinking about the impact on Jeff's family and the rest of the Trekkers. What impact was this going to have on the ride and the group. Would something drastic happen like stopping the ride at this point. I felt sorry for Gayle and Dave and all of the issues they would have to deal with in the next few hours and days. When I got to camp everyone was huddled in small groups talking, a few Trekkers were by themselves sitting against a wall or in a chair. The rest of the evening went by slowly and some of us basically stayed up waiting to hear what the plans were for the next day and the Trek overall. We were given a short briefing by Gayle and Dave and told that the ride would continue on in the morning. So we waited for sunrise and wanting to get on the road each dealing with their feelings in their own way.

(Mary Fleming #27) How do I write about this day? It was a tragic day. Yet it brought us together as a group and demonstrated forcefully the community that we have formed over the last five weeks. We had a thunderstorm overnight and it was still cool and drizzly when Jim and I left at 6;30 a.m. On leaving Valparaiso University we went up a hill to meet an overpass for Hwy 421. Very quickly, the shoulders on the road disappeared and we were riding on a two lane road which dropped of slightly to gravel shoulders at the white line. Within three miles of our starting point we saw some cars stopped and people walking across the road and knew something was wrong. I asked someone what had happened and was told that it was a hit and run accident. Two of our cyclists had been hit. Jerry and Jeff had been riding together, single file when a car hit Jeff with a great impact, throwing him beyond Jerry. The car then hit Jerry with less force. When we arrived, two or three people were working on Jeff I tried to give Jerry a hand. His primary injury was with his leg and some abrasions and he seemed to be going into shock. After awhile the Trek van arrived with medical supplies and our EMT's. An ambulance arrived soon after and took them both to the hospital. At that point there was nothing to do but ride on. I can't begin to describe what the ride was like or what kind of area we passed through. I am writing this all several days later when I could finally sit down and put pen to paper about the experience.

BIO LAURA REMALY #185

In 1989 I was working as a Director for a Corporate Fitness Company. For the year leading up to Trek, I was busy designing and setting up a new facility for a Bank's new Headquarters. It was a massive project and I spent a year working on the facility and hiring the staff needed to run it. In March or April of that year, I spoke to a dear friend of mine who was planning to go on a bike trip across the United States. Immediately I was jealous and said "Gee, I have always wanted to do that". He said " so, why don't you?" I mentioned the usual excuses - job, money, etc. But then the idea started eating away at me and I couldn't think of anything else. So, I asked my boss if I could go on the trip. I reminded her that I had worked for the company for over 10 years, had approximately 8 weeks of unused vacation saved up and had earned it due to my recent work. She replied that she didn't think that the timing was appropriate and that maybe they would consider letting me go next year. She said she would ask her supervisor and get back to me. By the time she got back to me I had already decided I was going no matter what, and luckily the company agreed to let me go and I didn't lose my job over it. Then came the hard part. I only had four weeks to raise $5,000, prepare my bike and supplies and get my affairs in order. I didn't quite raise all of the money I needed and put in some of my own but was thrilled to be on my way. I was already in pretty good condition because I was a competitive tri athlete at the time.

As a side note, I needed quite a bit of work on my bicycle before going on Trek, and the person who "worked on my bike for free as part of his sponsorship to me" became my husband two years later. If not for Trek, I never would have met my husband, Matt McGoey.

(Laura Remaly #185) This morning Jeff sat at the table next to me at breakfast, he was kind of quiet, but always smiling and laughing. I didn't get to know him to well yet but thought he was a sincere, jovial guy. We were some of the first people on the road that day. When I got to the accident, Greg Steele had just started CPR on him and Phil Torres and I helped him. Greg had a look of dread on his face - he knew our efforts were fruitless. I couldn't believe what was happening and didn't recognize him even though I had just seen him ten minutes before. I prefer to remember his smiling face as opposed to the lifeless figure left lying on the ground. I will always think back on that and remember that Jeff died doing what he loved and wouldn't want us to feel sorry for him. There is no better way to go.

(Hubert 'Woody" Wood #237) The worst day on Trek of course was the day Jeff Green died. Hearing on the road about the accident, then finding out details later was awful. I had ridden with Jeff a lot in the days before, so his death hurt even more. Trek was a life changing experience for me. It gave me the courage to make difficult life decisions, confidence to do things I had only dreamed of and probably the greatest feeling of satisfaction I will know.

(Nancy Eiselt #6) Today was by far everyone's most difficult day on Trek. Jerry kept on saying (weeks ago) that we hadn't had enough adversity to pull the group together, that we needed some hardship. Today that uniting occurred when disaster struck.

Janice and I awoke to a cool, drizzly morning. Neither of us had slept well. First the blasted heat, then the thunderstorm that started slamming doors up and down the hall of the dorm at Valparaiso University. My instinct was to sleep in a while, it being Sunday and rainy, but I knew the heat was expected today, so I forced myself to get up around 5:15 a.m. We dragged our bones to breakfast, lingered over a cup of coffee, then packed up and checked out.

Janice was waiting for me and said "Can you handle this?" Three people just got hit by a car." The van had just screamed out of the lot, and as we pedaled out we heard sirens in the distance. We chatted about the alleged accident, speculating as to who it might be. We felt certain it wasn't Karin and Guy, or Jeff and Jerry, as they had left long ago and the accident sounded close by.

As we took the exit off 30 onto SR49, the flashing lights were visible - lots of them. I thought it strange that anyone could possibly be hit by a car before 7 a.m. on Sunday, there was hardly any traffic. But my heart began racing. Who could it be?

We came upon Damian standing in the roadway. His first

words were "You don't want to go up there. It's bad" we asked who it was? "Jeff"he said "Which Jeff? Balding Jeff? We asked" Yes" was his reply.

I lost it. The tears poured out and sobs began. How bad? No one knew for sure, but it appeared serious. Janice and I walked up to the scene of the accident. Jeff and Jerry had been whisked away in aid cars already, but the news we got was grim. Jerry appeared to have a broken leg, but Jeff had sustained serious head injuries. Bruce Leonard had administered CPR until the aid cars arrived, but he said the weak pulse disappeared and never returned, and Jeff never took over his own breathing.

Then began the long, painful wait. Lots of tears, hugging and dazed reminiscing - not to mention the terrifying thought: What if I had left with them today, as I had several times during the past week? I expected the worst news, but no one would confirm anything. I refused to ride until I knew his condition. Karin and I returned to camp to continue our wait, while Janice and Bruce went to the hospital.

It was obvious that most of the folks back in camp had no idea what had happened. Karin and I tried to keep our emotions under control a little, but it was tough. Shortly before 10 a.m. we learned that Jeff had died,

I felt an indescribable sense of loss, anger, and grief. Jeff had been such a kind, witty and upbeat part of my last week. Visions of his face and of his great team Monopod "Forward .Putz!" routine kept flashing in my mind. To think he'd just been in Janice's and my room the previous night, shooting the breeze and trying to keep our minds off the heat. And he was gone. Just like that. I keep hearing him calling me, "Nurse Nancy." I think about our evening in Chicago, and I think about his family. His poor Mother worried incessantly about him on Trek. I had dreamed about Jeff and Janice last night, too, and Janice and I had gotten a good laugh out of that as were getting going this morning.

I kept wanting to see Janice, and she finally returned from the hospital. We held each other and cried some more. Then she said she wanted to ride. I was shaken, but figured that would be the best thing for me to do as well. So, shortly after 10:00, Janice, Bruce,

Sam Sylvester and I set out on the most difficult ride I've had. We had to pass the scene of the accident again - and I choked up again. There was still blood on the pavement.

The miles rolled away agonizingly slow, and the humidity and heat were already oppressive. Strong winds buffeted us, keeping us at a maximum speed of about 15 mph. We stopped several times and went through our crying spells, laughter, and quiet contemplation. Everyone's mood was, of course very heavy.

(Marianne Brems #49) Suddenly, so suddenly everything has become so real. Is death not more real than anything? In this heightened level of existence death too seems more real. We stood around and cried like babies. It reminds me of the time a man had a heart attack in the pool in Spokane at the nationals. It ever so quickly puts life into perspective. In fact, I think nothing puts life into perspective as quickly as death. Mother and Dad who came from Illinois to visit me took it more in stride than I thought they would. They were lounging around the lawn at the school when I came in for the day. A short but firm litany on the drawbacks of the highway followed. We had a refreshing swim in the pool, while Dad sat by and looked from under those eyebrows.

In the evening I saw fireflies. Robin talks to fireflies.

(Sharon White #291) When asked to describe the worst day on the Trek, everyone's answer is the same. After Valparaiso, Indiana, it was an affront to complain about broken spokes, flat tires, aches and pains. We were staying at the Valparaiso University - another tent-less treat the day after staying at Loyola College in Chicago.

The last time I saw Jeff Green, he was heading to the gear truck and I was heading out on the road. As was his style, he greeted me with his infectious smile and Texan "Mornin", Sharon. To this day, I feel a little wedge of warmth when I'm welcomed this way and similarly when I'm having the occasional bagel and lox. Jeff being Jewish and me as a quarter blood, albeit non-practicing Jew, lamented almost daily about how we couldn't find a decent bagel on the Trek. Or for that matter, a worthy cup of coffee, as this was the pre-Starbucks era. We had a long standing friendly ribbing about whether Montreal-style bagels were better than the New York variety. We mutually vowed to continue our trip on the east coast to New York and Quebec to settle the score. We also pledged to ride together more on the Trek, but both promises went unfulfilled.

That morning in Valparaiso I was surprised to see him off to a late start as me not being an early bird, he was always on the road first. In fact, a few days earlier we had ridden together for the first time in Chicago. A bunch of us took advantage of a day off to get to the windy city to catch a Cubs game. As a fledging sport writer, going to Wrigley Field to see the ivy and hear Harry Carey's grating yet legendary seventh inning stretch rendition of Take Me Out to The Ballgame was to me, nirvana with hot dogs and peanuts to boot. I don't know how, but Guy Smith somehow rustled up enough tickets for a group of us - Johnny, Jerry, a few of the seven Jeff's, myself and a few other sport fans. Jeff had a blast. We all did. I remember him saying something like "look here Sharon, were here in Wrigley field. Can you believe it? And I couldn't so I phoned my Dad back in Victoria for posterity or proof. Or God knows why. I just felt I had to tell somebody. Yes Jeff Green was in his element and I can't help but think that in the last few days of his too-short life, he was doing exactly what he was meant to do - having the time of his life ands inviting the rest of the world to share it with him.

I responded to Jeff's "Mornin Sharon": that day with an invitation to ride together. He told me not to wait, but to go ahead and we would catch up later on the road.

Apparently his ride out of Chicago the day before was riddled with flat tires and bad luck, so he was satisfied to enjoy a lazy start and set out with Jerry on his own behind the rest of us. I can't help but wonder if a more earnest urging on either of our part could have changed fate.His or mine.

I got to know Jeff as much as anybody else on Trek. His riding partner was Jerry and his best buddy was Janice - a gregarious Bostonian who had to leave the Trek a week after Jeff's death because her fiancé had a heart attack. Losing a great friend and worried about her fiancé was more stress than he deserved. She was a wonderful lady and did join us for the last few days of the Trek as we rode into New Jersey.

Sunrise 47

Back at the Valparaiso start, Jen and I headed out as usual. It would be difficult to describe the day in relationship to what happened without being cliché. The day itself was like a no other. The sky was gray heartless and depressing, uninspiring after weeks of sunshine and blue skies. There was a haze that would burn off later in the day, but the weather condition made an eventual bleak morning that much more miserable. In Indiana the roads were straight flat and unexceptional. After weeks of hills and wind, it was surprising to see so many Trekkers stopped at a drive-in restaurant about 20 miles into the day's schedule. Everyone had stopped. Even the keeners who stopped for nothing. Everybody sat quietly on the restaurants picnic tables. It was too early for lunch and the restaurant owners didn't dare drive anyone out. As each Trekker arrived at the drive-in someone would quietly take him or her aside and tell them the news. Johnny and Fargo Jeff took Jen and me aside. There's been an accident," Johnny said. "A car hit Jerry and Jeff.He didn't have to explain which Jeff as everybody knew Jeff and Jerry were riding buddies. Jerry was taken away with a broken leg, Johnny continued, "Jeff didn't make it."

It took a few seconds to realize exactly what "didn't make it" meant. It was a phrase meant to be used to explain someone missing an appointment or a flight. When Johnny's words finally registered, they hit hard. I immediately thought about Jeff's family. Nine years earlier, my brother had been killed in a car accident, so I knew that within hours there would be a phone call or a police visit to Jeff's parents with the news., News that is so unbelievable, but painfully real.

I don't know how or when we got back on our bikes that day - some didn't. We knew that Jeff was killed by a hit and run driver, but we didn't know much more. Spooked by any unusual noise or movement, we cautiously and mechanically rode. I desperately wanted to phone home, but every available phone booth lining the route was busy with Trekkers calling home to tell loved ones what happened and that they were okay. Living in Victoria, so close to the Seattle start, I didn't know if the accident would make the KING or KOMO TV news that evening. I certainly didn't want my family to learn the news that way. Our riding group stopped for lunch at a restaurant in a small, friendly town a few hours later. Waiting for my grilled cheese sandwich (my comfort food) I was finally able to phone home to tell Mom the news. When I got back to the table, an elderly couple was asking us about our bike ride. Unbelievably they asked us if we had experienced any crazy drivers. Jen and I looked at each other and nodded a quick no.

(Nancy Ackles #124) I remember extremely well the church that invited us to worship with them on the Sunday morning that Jeff died. I arrived just as the service was beginning and the usher looked at my cycling gear and said, "We're so sorry about your loss." He seated me in a side section very near the front. There were a couple of young fathers with their son's in the only pew in front of me. The hymn number was announced, and suddenly from behind me came rich, four part harmony of a hymn full of whole notes and words, "Who bears our every woe, Christ the crucified." The sermon text was John 14, and while the sermon wasn't directed right at us, we were included. I remember the pastor saying that Christ was on a journey and many of us, to, were on a journey and didn't know how it would end. The sermon included Christ, sin, salvation, and heaven, not harsh but graciously and warmly preached. Then at the end, the pastor spoke directly to our situation and said, "We don't know anything about Jeff Green, about his background or life experience. But we know that his hope was the same as our hope, because God's love is universal.

Then it was time for announcements and the man making them said that their community too had received those awful phone calls like the one Jeff's parents received. He asked us to accept their offer of whatever we needed just then. The pastor asked if anyone could remember the hymn number for "What a friend we have in Jesus" and again the rich four part harmony swelled.

The service was over, and as I stood I could at last look back and see the congregation. All the men sat on one side and the women on the other.(therefore the fathers in front of me. I had entered on the men's side). They sang a cappella harmony because they didn't allow any musical instruments in worship. The women all had both their head and arms covered. Trekker's didn't even have their bodies covered much less their heads. But we stood among those people and were loved. They offered phones comforting words, and help. And then we got on our bikes and left, like a small flock of birds who suddenly landed in distress and then took off, never to be seen again.

(Karin Allen #29) It had been a stormy night, so I hadn't slept well and found myself awake very early. I ran into Guy at breakfast and we decided to ride together, even though we'd had a run of bad luck on our last two outings (our wreck and Terri's). We started up a quiet country highway very early in the morning (around 6:30 or so) and hadn't gone far when I saw a bike in the road, with one of the wheels bent into a Pac-Man shape. Clearly the bike had been hit by a car, but I didn't see anyone until I looked further up the road, and there was Jerry Wright, with an injured leg, yelling at us to "find the yellow car and help Jeff". That's when I saw Jeff lying in a pool of blood. Riders Damian and Bruce were already trying to help Jeff, but I was in a complete panic. I was shaking and crying and found myself unable to be of any help whatsoever except to help direct traffic around the accident scene. Within minutes, the scene was swarming with a number of healthcare professionals, both from the Trek and locals. Guy and I cried and held on to each other, but I became even more agitated when they took Jerry away but the ambulance with Jeff in it just sat in place. I couldn't help wondering, why are they still here? They should be racing him to the hospital.

I returned to Valparaiso University and waited for word on Jeff. Once they told us he had died, I became hysterical. I wanted to go home immediately. I called my boyfriend who was incredibly supportive, but he suggested I talk to my parents. When I called my parents I was surprised when they strongly urged me to stay on the ride. They told me although I had been incredibly fortunate so far in my life, terrible things sometimes happen, and a true test of who you are as a human being is how you face those challenges. They said it was important that I stay to support the rest of the Trekkers. It was then that I realized although I had not been able to help Jeff at the accident scene, I could help the rest of the group and myself by staying and working through our grief together. Guy and I went to church in our bike gear and stood in the back and cried. Then we were driven to the midday check point - the first and only time I had sagged the entire trip. By the time I had spent several hours talking to riders as they came in and helping them (and me) deal with the grief, I knew no matter what, I had to go on. At the time, I couldn't believe I had the strength or the will, but I found myself thinking that Jeff would have wanted us to go on. That thought, combined with my parent's and my boyfriend's input, gave me the determination to finish the Trek.

Day 36 Delphi Indiana to Indianapolis Indiana 68 miles as remembered by Trekkers Guy Smith #280, Mary Fleming #27 and Nancy Eislet #6

(**Guy Smith #280**) My bike frame was broken beyond repair. Craig, the mechanic promised me that he'd take it to a dealer in Indianapolis to get a new one. Meanwhile he adjusted one of the staff mountain bikes for me so that it would be suitable for the 68 mile trip to Indianapolis. Against the advice of the medical staff, Terri decided to ride also. Her face, shoulders, and chest were covered with bandages. Though this was a short mileage day on level roads, it was a huge challenge for this brave woman. We decided to ride together. Meanwhile, the trip was apparently over for Jerry; but he decided to stay with the Trek for awhile, at least until after the memorial service for Jeff, planned for our evening in Zaneville, Ohio, four days down the road. Very early in the morning it was cool, but as soon as the sun came up the temperature and the humidity started to climb. Another rough day was in store but each of us prayed that it would be a "normal day". On the road Trekker's were quiet and somber, many rode alone and occasionally someone sang "Roi's" song or even wept. Young Damian from Great Britain was sitting alongside the road weeping bitterly. We found out later that he was riding right behind Jeff and Jerry on Sunday and was the first one to reach Jeff and tried desperately to save his life with the basic ABC's of first aid (Airway, Breathing and Circulation) He got comfort from Michelle who spotted him there beside the road, and the two became close friends. The mid-day checkpoint at Lebanon was a somber gathering. Even when a large group of us stopped at a Dairy Queen to get Terri some blizzard energy, nobody dared laugh even when something funny happened. It just doesn't feel right to laugh. Terri should have quit at the checkpoint but she went on. The afternoon became more and more difficult for her. Her energy level was low, since she could only eat liquids. She had to stop to drink, since she was unable to maneuver her water bottle around the bandages on her face. The bandages started coming loose and wouldn't stick. She was afraid to leave any skin uncovered for fear that infection would cause scarring on her face. It became harder and harder to get her to stop to drink and I was worried about dehydration. She was drinking only one fourth of my consumption. You can imagine her frustration when we missed a crucial turn in Indianapolis and had to ride several extra miles to get to our destination at Marian College. When we finally arrived, without a word to anyone, she made a beeline to the dorm to rest. When I signed in at the blue bus, the rolling administrative headquarters of the Trek I was surprised by more visitors. Paul's wife Pat and the three girls (Angela, Faith and Tera) were there to greet me. They had heard of Jeff's accident through the Smith family grapevine and had driven up from Cincinnati to comfort me. It was such a warm and caring thing to do. They treated me to dinner at the Olive Garden Italian restaurant, famous for its great pasta. Being with children again gave me a better insight into life. They were so full of vitality that I could feel the joy of living rebuilding inside me despite the tragedy. The young girls donated generously to Jeff's fund and met the Trekker's, sharing their joy of youth with everyone. Meanwhile Craig had taken my bike to the Raleigh dealer in Indianapolis and had gotten me a new frame, free of charge because the other one was only four months old. I suspect he didn't mention that I had ridden it 4,300 miles since I purchased it on April 1st. Craig, the miracle man promised me that my new bike would be ready to roll by early morning.I fell asleep with a prayer of thanks for the normal day.

(Mary Fleming #27) This day was a blur. I believe we went through some rather nice country with a river and some vacation spots but all I can remember was encountering some irate and inconsiderate drivers and feeling frightened of being on the road.

(**Nancy Eislet #6**) I chose to ride alone today and did more crying on the road. Several times I was choked by sobs I don't know what prompted my spells, but the tear reservoir had been refilled overnight and I shed some more. I remember two instances: one when I began singing "Amazing Grace" and felt just like I did at Marilyn's (my sister-in-law) funeral. The sorrow reached so far into me I could barely get the words out. The other instance was when a row of about four semis started passing a slower moving truck that was in the oncoming lane. For some reason, seeing the semis coming down the road toward me in my lane really shook me up. I pulled off into the gravel and cried.

Day 37 Indianapolis Indiana to Richmond Indiana 85 miles as remembered by Trekkers Guy Smith #280, Hal Laster #16 and Marianne Brems #49

(**Guy Smith #280**)This morning was delightfully cool as I joined Marie from Washington and Barbara from Monterey, CA for the day's ride. I had wanted to ride with Marie for a long time, feeling a kinship to her lively personality and deep sense of spirituality. We shared thoughts and ideas with intensity as we rode along, first through the lovely grounds of a US Army Post and then through the flat farmlands of Eastern Indiana. Craig had done a beautiful job on my bike and it performed superbly. The details of the day's ride were lost because I was more interested in sharing with Marie. Our conversation went back and forth all day from deeply philosophical to childlike simplicity. We even laughed, and it felt good. The ride came to an end to quickly. As we entered the spacious Glen Miller Park in Richmond I became aware that a van was following us with a TV camera. It was my brother, Paul, who is a producer of the PBS-TV show, "For Veterans Only" I had arranged for some interviews with military vets on the Trek that Paul wanted us to use in his show. His time to do filming and interviews was very limited, so we set to work filming riders along the road talking to former military people as they rode in. Later all of this was edited to a five minute segment that aired on more than 200

Sunrise 47

PBS stations, in the US and on the Armed forces overseas network. Paul and Joe his videographer, left early in the evening. That evening a local psychologist had been invited to meet with all the Trekkers and staff who had been on the scene of Jeff and Jerry's accident. He skillfully guided the session as each one told their version of the story. Jerry was almost in a trance as he relived the moment by moment. Until then nobody had realized the internal anguish of Damian, the first person on the scene, who tried all he could to save Jeff's life. Bruce the man from New Mexico who had performed CPR on Jeff emerged as a strong leader of our group, and was asked to help organize a memorial service for Jeff in Zanesville. Karen and I got our turn to tell our story and to recall our feelings of total helplessness. There was a lot of hugging and crying in this small group. Meeting in the dim light of a park shelter. When it broke up around midnight a great deal of healing had taken place. But it was hard to fall asleep, as a distant siren wailed in the night across the city of Richmond stirring up images in our dreams.

(Hal Laster #16) One of my best days....I just really felt strong today and thanks to a quiet Indiana breeze, I just propelled faster than I had ever ridden. And I don't know why, but I rode solo that day - maybe because my riding buddies didn't want to hurry that day and I did because my American Lung Association sponsor from Cincinnati was going to meet me in camp. So I just rode on without them. I remember experiencing the "riders high" or the 'zone" that day - when your pedaling and nothing can slow you down. I think I was the third or fourth cyclist into camp - whereas, I was usually one of the last. It was such a funny site - to arrive into camp ahead of our gear truck, and to see the site with NO tents setup. That was a one and only experience.

(Marianne Brems #49) The heat is the topic of the day. Everyone is affected. I felt shaky at the end of the ride, even giddy a little bit but then the temperature dropped at least 15 degrees and everyone's mood changed. There was also a feeling of pleasant reunion with the showers. One woman said "Here we are among our own germs, not 300 college students germs that we've never even seen". Others said "We'll take Cascade anytime".

There was a meeting to talk about the accident with Jerry and Jeff, but it didn't seem to me there was the emotion that I heard there the night it happened. People were working out their own stuff more than being involved with the loss of Jeff.

Chapter 8

Day 38 Richmond Indiana to Columbus Ohio 100 miles as remembered by Trekkers Guy Smith #280, Gordon Croft #250, Ellen Lowe #42 and Marianne Brems #49

(**Guy Smith #280**) I was awake by 4:00 a.m. and started preparing for our 101 mile trip to Columbus Ohio, our last century ride of the Trek. I woke Karin up, and we decided to skip breakfast at camp in order to get a few miles under our belt while it was cool. On the message board in front of the blue bus was some good news. Back in Valparaiso, they had arrested a 20 year old, Andrew Barlog, a security guard at a Gary, Indiana steel mill who fell asleep at the wheel of his car when he hit Jerry and Jeff. Barlog had admitted to hitting the cyclists stating that he ran away because he was scared. To us it was comforting to know that the hit and run driver had been found. At 2.5 miles into the day we crossed into Ohio, taking pictures with 59 year old Dottie Potts, a grandmother and a native of Ohio She told us to be sure to stop at Philipsburg, where her townsfolk's would be throwing a party. Dottie was one of the Trek hero's. She was usually one of the first Trekker's on the road in the early morning and one of the last to arrive at camp at night. Her pace was slow but never faltering and she never complained, just rode along singing her songs and saying hello to each Trekker as they passed her. We were glad to be in Ohio, though we lost an hour passing into the Eastern Time Zone Leaving Indiana behind meant placing some distance between us and the events that happened there. Karen and I talked about these things and about life as we rode along the quite farm roads. After 24 miles we stopped in Verona for breakfast and shocked the waitress that both of us could eat the equivalent of two meals. We were still full when we came upon the celebration for Dottie at Phillipsburg. We didn't dare ride past because the entire town was there to welcome us with cheers, balloons, banners and homemade cookies for everyone. Later in the morning Karen narrowly missed being hit by a car; and when she broke down and sobbed, I knew that she was also crying for Jeff. We got caught in a summer shower at the checkpoint town of Springfield, but in the wake of that storm we picked up a strong tail wind which propelled us along the last 3 miles of the day. A tail wind is a very special friend of the Trekker's and I marveled how timely it was on this century day and how it uplifted our spirits so much. That day there was laughter and fun as the joyful spirit of the Trek started to return. Arriving at the Wetland High School in West Columbus, I had more company, my niece, Julaine, and her college boyfriend, Doug, were there to greet me. People began to wonder if I had relatives in every city in the East. Julaine and Doug helped us do our laundry and met new friends as they shared dinner with us at the high school. That evening a group of us, led by Bruce, met to plan Jeff's memorial service. We decided to make it very upbeat a celebration of Jeff's life. We asked for volunteers to contribute songs, poems and stories for the occasion. Hal the Assistant Dean of the Cincinnati Music Conservatory, organized a Trekker choir, the first ever in the history of Transamerica bicycle trekking. One puzzle about organizing the celebration was how to end it. We decided to let anyone who wished to come forward and share their thoughts. We would let the ending happen spontaneously.

(**Gordon Croft #250**) While in Chicago I bought a pair of Look Pedals. You have to twist out of them to put a foot on the ground. In Columbus Ohio, as we were in rush hour traffic, I came to a stoplight with another rider, and again forgot to twist before putting my foot down on the ground. I put my right hand out for support on the other rider and brought us both to the ground. He never rode near me again, but I'm sure he remembers me. I got rid of the Look Pedals and have since gone to the much improved Shimano system. My apologize to that rider again.

(**Ellen Lowe #42**) I remember Dottie Potts who wore light weight red, white or blue cotton tights (not cycling tights) everyday to keep her legs from getting sunburned. When we passed through her small town of Laura, she was treated like returning royalty. Dottie's reception was complete with a huge brass band and a parade with Dottie out front, of course, along with siren blaring fire trucks.

(**Marianne Brems #49**) We're back to the small town feeling of lemonade stands and friendly waves. I think.

I think people are glad to be out of Indiana. Today was a good ride for most people because the roads were sparsely traveled. The fourth of July house was the highlight of the day. Complete with a tape of the tenants.

Day 39 Columbus Ohio to Zanesville Ohio 67 miles as remembered by Trekker's Mary Fleming #27, Guy Smith #280, Hal Laster #16, Nancy Eislet #6 and Marianne Brems #49

(**Hal Laster #16**) My Son and a friend came up from Cincinnati to see me last night and this morning when I left camp they had put up a sign as we left the high school parking lot "Good Luck TEAM SLOW.... Don't fall off the Boardwalk." I still have the sign.

(**Mary Fleming #27**) One more riding day and we get our last rest day. After that only 6 more riding days. The trip is coming to an end very soon. I have mixed feelings about the end. It means time to go home and face reality again, make decisions and get on with my life. I will end up wishing I had done more with the trip and taken fuller advantage of all of the activities, etc., spent more time establishing people contacts, seen more of the off-road sites. Unfortunately, I have a limited amount of energy at the end of each day.

(**Marianne Brems #49**) Smug as a bug in a rug. Risks and rewards. Nikki's song about hugs.

Dealing with this loss of Jeff is a really complex process. So many emotions fly around and there are so many questions. The group is pulling together. Would they have anyway? I don't know. The group felt like it was connected to the tragedy. People were more philosophical and less grief stricken. But also they were more hopeful and willing to recognize the positive outcome (the bonding). They were willing to make it part of their life's experience. They were willing to touch too, but not so much out of desperation as before.

(Guy Smith #280) The trip to Zanesville was a short mileage day, but most Trekker's except Ohio natives, didn't know about the steep hills in Eastern Ohio. We had been spoiled by the flat terrain; we hadn't climbed a hill since Eastern Wisconsin. I rode with a large group right through the city of Columbus, the busy capital city of Ohio. After the checkpoint city of Hebron, I rode with Michelle and Cam up and down the hilly and scenic country roads. Cam was one of the most improved riders of the Trek; in the early going she was fairly slow, but now she rode steady and strong on these challenging roads. About 15 miles from Zanesville I ran out of gas. It' called "bonking", when the body runs out of energy and nothing works. But Cam and Michelle were still strong and I drafted them into town where we found a pizza place to replenish my energy supply. We camped that night on the grounds of the Bethesda City hospital. My first concern was to help set up for the "Celebration of Jeff's Life" at a large picnic shelter. After dinner we assembled there. The service was just what we hoped for- a real celebration of Jeff and of being alive. As master of ceremonies, Bruce was magnificent, mixing emotional moments with light ones.

There were songs, poems, prayers, stories and even laughter. One of the most memorable moments was the singing of "May the Good Lord Bless and Keep You" in four-part harmony by the Trekker choir and "Kumbaya" by the choir and the whole assembly. Lou's toothless grin was priceless when he got a standing ovation for his harmonica solo.Marty from Georgia had designed a special Jeff Green button which were passed out to everyone by "Team Jeff Minus One" on their bicycle helmets. It was 11:00 p.m. and thing were still going strong when Nikki from Minnesota got up with her guitar and offered to sing a song about hugs that she made up several years before. By the time she got to verse six, people were on their feet hugging each other. She never got a chance to finish her song before she too was in the middle of a hug fest. Hugging, crying, and laughing went on into the night. Jeff's vibrant and fun filled spirit was alive among us, and the healing and peace it brought us was very strong and noticeable.

(Nancy Eislet #6) What a magical celebration we just had for Jeff. Bruce did an excellent job of expressing how bittersweet is the feeling of having to wait for a tragedy like Jeff's death to bring us together. He urged us all to risk in the next week to reach out to people we don't know, to make a miracle happen in this group as a tribute to Jeff. He mentioned that Jeff's best friend told Bruce on the phone today that "Jeff was a gatherer of people. He had a special ability to get along with all kinds of people, to bring them together". Perhaps his death was just a further extension of that quality - the bringing together of this group that had been somewhat distant because of the lack of strife.

Chapter 9

Day 40 Zanesville Ohio to Wheeling West Virginia 88 miles as remembered by Trekker's Guy Smith #280, Mary Fleming #27, Mike Mitchell #1, Ellen Lowe #42 and Marianne Brems #49

(Guy Smith #280) Today my spirits were low and melancholy. Preparing for the celebration service and trying to help others deal with their feelings had taken its toll. I needed to be alone to think about my own feelings and to come to grips with my own life. For the first time I started to think about life and the Trek. With only one week remaining the end seemed to be in sight, and I had to start thinking about my future. The big steep rolling hills were the perfect setting for introspection. The weather was merciful - it was warm and dry. The country roads were beautiful with virtually no traffic. Just when my leg muscles were rebelling against the hills, the road leveled off and followed a railroad line through the valley. I spent no time at all at the mid-day checkpoint; I just wanted to be alone with my thoughts. Even when I stopped at a Dairy Queen for a blizzard, I was without the usual boisterous crowd. Crossing the Ohio river into West Virginia, I realized that these were no longer hills, we were in the Appalachian Mountains, the last major challenge of the Trek. But first we had a real weekend in Wheeling our last layover town. I set up my tent under a tall shade tree on the lovely grounds of the Linsly school, a wealthy private boys school that strongly contrasted with the industrial poverty of this city. The Lung Association of Wheeling gave us the best reception of the Trek. Their enthusiastic welcoming committee cheered as each Trekker arrived and gave us free t-shirts, information packets, fresh fruit throughout the weekend, and mail. I always seemed to have more mail than anyone else, a tribute to my big supportive family and wonderful sponsors. Supper was a banquet shared with some people who were being helped by the efforts of the local Lung Association. Before going to bed I went to a bar to dance. Normally I don't frequent bars, but on Trek it was so much fun because I knew so many people, and I love to dance.

(**Mary Fleming #27**) In Zanesville, we stayed on the grounds of the Bethesda hospital. Dinner was a Mexican buffet and breakfast was really good hospital cafeteria food.

We had a memorial service for Jeff last night. He was Jewish, so they started with two other Jewish Trekkers describing typical Jewish customs that occur with a family death. They recited in English and in Hebrew a prayer that the family would repeat during the year of mourning.

(**Mike Mitchell #1**) As was my normal pattern for the majority of the trip I rode most of the day by myself. I usually ride for short periods of time with a few of the Trekkers maybe 5 or 10 miles and either fall behind or pull ahead. The memorial for Jeff last night was very emotional. I am thinking more and more about my granddaughter Lindsey and the battle she is putting up. She is now in a coma. I am hopping for the best but it doesn't sound good. Obviously I am depressed and will probably have to get a few hugs when I get to camp tonight.

(Ellen Lowe #42) I remember Bob Carson and Hugh Harold were comparing birthdates to determine who could claim the distinction of being the oldest Trekker. Hugh was just a couple of months younger than Bob. So, Hugh started calling Bob, Dad and in turn Bob called Hugh, son. Turns out the oldest honors went to Lou Trantales with Bob second and Hugh third,

(Marianne Brems #49) People are happy again. There really isn't any need for a tug-of-war or a water fight. People have processed their grief in a very real way. Again everything seems so heightened and the stages of things accelerated. This is so because we are such an isolated community. Here no one is an employee, or a parent, or a board member or any such thing. The first day (the day of Jeff's death) people grieved openly and held onto each other. The next few days people were just unhappy and complained about unimportant things. Then we had the celebration of life and people's spirits were lifted with the help of the whole group. Again a lot of hugging.

Day 41 Wheeling West Virginia Rest Day 0 miles as remembered by Trekker's Guy Smith #280 and Joanne, Steve Andersen #109 and Marianne Brems #49

BIO STEVE ANDERSEN #109

I would like to share a letter with everyone that I received from Joanne Andersen the wife of Trekker #109 Steve Andersen. Joanne said, "In 1988 Steve was diagnosed with an illness called "Machado Joseph" disease. It causes loss of cells in the balance and coordination part of the brain. Steve was laid off on disability in June 1988 faced with the job of making the most of the time he would be able-bodied. Steve wanted to do something really significant, something so special that someday when the disease had taken a lot away from him he could "look out the window and remember" what a fantastic adventure he had had

(Steve Andersen #109) Steve was drawn to serious bicycle riding by his brother-in-law, Leonard, as well as living in Iowa where the RAGBRAI attracts over 10,000 riders each July. Steve

Sunrise 47

rode in the Register's Annual Great Bike Ride across Iowa a couple of times, whetting his appetite for a major trip across the whole country.

Translating the Great Idea into a concrete plan and successful journey was a huge pile of difficult questions. Thankfully early in the planning process, an item in the newspaper caught his eye. A meeting for bicyclists interested in the American Lung Association Transamerica Bicycle Trek 89 was being held in Des Moines, 200 miles from home. That meeting provided all the answers to the pile of questions - when to go, where to go, what to pack, how to get from here to there. They took care of logistics, leaving Steve free to concentrate on training.

I don't know what it was to experience and accomplish the TA Trek of 89 "You had to be there". I can be a reporter and share what I observed of Steve's life as a Trekker.

Early in the mountains of Washington, the bike had it's first breakdown. After a long hard ride up the mountain, he made it to Steven's pass. Time to rest and anticipate the awesome ride downhill to follow. The long uphill climbs were amazingly difficult for Steve taking so much strength and power. When Steve dismounted to rest, the handlebar broke off at the frame. We are all very grateful it happened when it did.

Glacier National Park will always be next to heaven for Steve. That day-off from riding was timed perfectly in a beautiful locale. He was to the point of being so exhausted that he thought he couldn't go on. So many mountains, so many miles. Then came a day of resting and playing - recharging and all things were again possible.

The day the family at home heard little about was the day of the camper incident. The door of a travel trailer which was passing the Trek riders came open, hitting Steve and knocking him into a ditch. A heart stopping moment to witness by his fellow Trekker's. Blessedly, that's about the end of the story. Steve was OK except for bumps and bruises and a very dented helmet. He says he kept on riding that day.

When I told Steve I was writing some memories of Trek 89 and something you asked to hear about was the "best day of Trek", he told me "Going to the Sun Road with Roger" I asked was it the fantastic scenery? The perfect riding conditions? The marvelous people you were riding with" He answered "Yes".

Thanks to so many people, Steve completed the Trek. As they approached the eastern part of the country, the complications of the denser population were formidable, more people, more traffic, more roads to get lost on. Steve spoke of leaving Trek for safety reasons. However, the Trek family would have none of that after coming that distance together. Someone who owned a tandem bike agreed to loan it to Steve for the rest of the journey. The tandem was shipped in. The mechanics set it up for Steve and Roger to ride. Roger gave up his bike and agreed to ride the lead with Steve on through to Atlantic City. The Trekkers are an awesome group of people.

The hugs I shared with Steve and Roger on the boardwalk were awesome.

Steve lives at home these days with 5 of us helping him with his daily activities. He's positive and helpful to the best of his ability even though MJD has taken away his power to care for himself. We all try to count our blessings and love one another as gifts to each other.

(Marianne Brems #49) A perfect day! I got up when I felt like it. Go swim. Go eat. Clean my bike. Go to the water slide. Perfect weather.

Donna gave me a nice hair cut. I feel marginally more ready for Atlantic City now that I'm mended, cleaned, rested, trimmed and organized (somewhat)

(Guy Smith #280) Saturday was our last rest day before the big push into Atlantic City. The events of the previous week had taken its toll, and I really did sleep late that morning, even after the sun was high in the sky. I did the usual things for the rest day - writing post cards, doing laundry, cleaning bikes, and chatting. But in the afternoon I did a very strange thing indeed - I rode my bike. A group of us decided to ride some miles that day and donate them to the mileage fund for Jeff so that his ride would be finished for his sponsors. It wasn't a long ride (about 20 miles) and the day was beautiful. We rode to Ogelbay Park, a large city park with a golf

Sunrise 47

course, hiking trails, swimming pool, and lots of green hills. We swam and relaxed in the sun before returning to Linsly School for supper I went to bed early, anticipating a rough day in the mountains on Sunday.

Chapter 10

Day 42 Wheeling WV to Ohiopyle WV 90 miles as remembered by Trekker's Guy Smith #280, Mike Mitchell #1, Kevin Collins # 25, Nancy Ackles #124 and Marianne Brems #49

(Guy Smith #280) On Sunday I rode with Lisa Janisse from California. We had met in the early days of the Trek and had fun with our names, since my first name is French and her last name is Janisse. We had decided to switch names every Sunday, so on this day, like the six previous Sundays, I was Guy Janisse and she was Lisa Smith. Together we tackled the hills, most of the roads were steep and curvy but traffic early in the day was very light. Of course, we stopped for pictures at the "Welcome to Pennsylvania" sign, realizing that this was the last state to cross before New Jersey and the end of the Trek. At the midday checkpoint in Waynesburg we got a taste of Pennsylvania hospitality, a sumptuous feast was served to us by teenage beauty queens who were competing for the title of "Miss Rain Day" The rain day festival is a big event in this farming community, and their beauty queens made us all feel like royalty. But their great food was quickly used up in the laborious climbs, and we stopped again in Hopwood. Just ahead of us rose Laurel Ridge, a steep 3 mile hill covered with an ominous black cloud. We laughingly concluded that there must be a great car wash up there, because every car was dripping wet coming down from the mountain. Not far up the steep climb it began raining hard, and our soaked clothing made the climb very difficult. It was our introduction to the Appalachian Mountain Roads, much steeper than in the Rockies, because they don't use switchbacks to ease the grade. At times Lisa had to walk her bike up the hill because she had a racing bike which doesn't have a granny gear, the

very low ratio chain that permits a road bike to climb a steep grade at about 6 mph. I waited for her at the top but I got so chilled that my teeth started chattering. The steep downhill was treacherous in the rain, already two cyclists had taken spills but were not seriously injured. Highway traffic was now bumper to bumper along US 40 with weekend travelers returning home. It was a tremendous relief to turn off the main road onto a state highway, but it was difficult to fully enjoy the lush scenery with the heavy rain and the steep hills. We almost rode by the "3000 miles" sign painted on the roadway, but it was to important a milestone to miss. Only 360 miles to go; it seemed so short compared to the 3000 miles stretched behind us. It was almost dark when Lisa and I arrived at the campground at Ohipyle State Park. It took skill to put up tents in the pouring rain without getting everything totally wet. Some decided to skip it and rode eight extra miles into town and stayed in a hotel. The lasagna dinner was magnificent, and hot drinks were the order of the day. It was still early, but I decided that the only warm place was my sleeping bag. That night the rain truly tested the waterproofing on my tent, by morning everything was completely wet.

(Nancy Ackles #124) Today in the rain I thought maybe I'll just take a ride in the sag wagon when I get to the next checkpoint. But there wasn't a van at check point, and I kept riding. It was great to be able to say at the end that I'd made it all the way across country pedaling every step of the way myself.

(Mike Mitchell #1) I had been warned that the Appalachians sneak up on you. At some point in Ohio I noticed the farmland wasn't flat anymore. But before we hit those really big climbs there were great things to see. I especially enjoyed going thru Amish country and rode beside a horse cart for about a mile. I don't think the children inside were suppose to talk to me but they kept poking their heads out and smiling. I guess I got distracted and wasn't taking in fluids all morning. This was to hit me hard in the afternoon resulting in a trip to the hospital. After the second climb we had a rest stop at a restaurant. I hit the wall and went inside and lay down on a bench and fell asleep. Elaine woke me up and suggested that I eat and drink something. I didn't want to move but forced nourishment. I still didn't feel well when I got back on my bike. I managed to get up the next climb and then faced the Tuscarora mountain I was in granny and barely moving but was determined to get to the top and looked forward to coasting down the backside. I remember seeing the summit ahead and some staff people running around and then I went blank. The story that I got from one of the Trekker's behind me was that I just fell over and passed out. The next thing I really remember is being in a hospital with a IV in my arm and I was getting fluids. I stayed there for about two hours and then got in the van and was driven to camp. Dehydration is a bad thing and it took about three days to fully recover even though I was able to ride. Didn't feel like setting up my tent in the rain so I slept in a bathroom/sauna and had a horrible night.

(**Kevin Collins #25**) I think my worst day on the Trek was our ride to Ohiopyle. It was a rainy day and I did some good today helping fix a few flat tires. Making these stops to help made for a long day and I got into camp at the end of the pack. All that was left for dinner was a cold hamburger. I then found a nice saturated piece of land to camp out on but as I was setting up when a pole on my tent broke. That took care of camping out. I ended up sleeping in a shelter that included the bathrooms. The area was like a sauna and I don't think anyone slept.

(**Marianne Brems #49**)AM-a good feeling of a clean bike, cut hair and refreshed legs after a day of rest. Then came a bent rim, getting lost, another flat tire, and Robin's crash. It all goes to make you feel so vulnerable. Thank god were safe.

The rain makes things harder and takes longer. It's nice to be cool and have good sleeping weather. I was thinking today, I don't want to party when I get home. I just want to be left alone. I don't want to try to explain this experience to anyone. How can I? It's mine, no one else's.

Day 43 Ohlopyle PA to Bedford PA 76 miles as remembered by Trekker's Guy Smith #280, Gordon Croft #250, Nancy Eislet # 6, Woody Wood #237 and Marianne Brems #49

(**Marianne Brems #49**) The Trek experience is only what it is because of what we bring to it from the outside. If we hadn't learned language, vocabulary, and the ability to process information etc. we wouldn't feel so deeply. So I want to respect the importance of real life.

(**Guy Smith #280**) It had stopped raining. It was a wet, cool morning with a heavy overcast as I walked my bike through the woods, a shortcut that took us to the Great Gorge Bike Trail. Part of the 'Rails to Trails" system. I rode by myself again, not melancholy this time, just enjoying the early start and the coolness of the bike trail The scenery was spectacular as the trail crossed the Great Gorge carved out by the Youghiogheny River as it wound its way over the mountain. After 11 miles the bike trail ended and I was back on paved roads and back to climbing steep hills. I was having a ball going downhill, each time reaching about 45 mph. That day I was riding at the very front of the Trek, the riders there are more intense and less social. I didn't care. Hills are very personal, and it is often difficult to ride hills with somebody else who has a different style. I like to climb at a reasonably fast tempo and then go downhill as fast as possible. I arrived in Bedford early in the afternoon and had time to tour this colonial town, especially the Covered Bridge Museum. When I was putting up my tent, some local kids came around asking for autographs. They said, "If you ever win the Tour de France, we want to have your signature." of course I didn't tell them how improbable that was, but they loved the Colorado souvenir buttons I gave them. Dinner was great, but early in the evening, about ten of us took a walk to Howard Johnson's for a sundae before bed.

BIO GORDON CRAFT #250

In 1989 when I signed up for Trans Am, I was a 57 year old

engineer at Bell Laboratories working on telephone switching systems, living in Geneva, Illinois, somewhat addicted to adventures like wilderness canoeing, fishing and amateur mountain climbing. At the start of our TransAm adventure, I had been biking seriously for about eight years, done three cross-state Iowa "RAGBRAI" rides and two

Similar Illinois "BAMMIS" and maybe one or two Arizona "GABA's". Even not knowing anyone else who would do this, I thought I was ready for the challenge of TransAm.

NOTE: *Here is a Trekker account of that day when he seemed to have a special surge of energy and tried to do something that he wouldn't normally attempt. Most all of us experienced a similar experience along the way.*

(Gordon Craft #250) I found myself coming out of a Dairy Queen following my usual mid-afternoon milkshake, right behind "Team Extreme" that group of our younger people in their early 20's who rode hard during the day and partied hard in the evenings. The back of their T-Shirts said "If your gonna be tough, you gotta be stupid". Although being one of the fifteen or so people over 55, I knew most of "Team Extreme" (they're not unfriendly), but was clearly not one of them. We all fell in line riding the shoulders of the rural Pennsylvania roads. Having been doing this for six weeks, I had no trouble keeping up, there we were riding single file, first the boys/men then the girls/women and then me. Feeling a bit charged up after my milkshake, I experimented peddling slightly harder, passing some of the girls, then all of them. As I passed the front-most girl, I saw her glance sideways to see who this grizzled person was and heard her mumble under labored breathing "Oh s-t". I simply continued now passing some of the boys - there wasn't any place to pull back in line - until I came to the head of the line with those two Marines who were on detached duty for physical training, you know with the close-cropped crew cuts, tough as nails, and attitude to match, and then Tom Canisi, Boston sewer construction worker, who was even bigger of musculature. Passing by I somehow felt the need for explanation, and so I said to Tom "My bike just doesn't want to go this slow" and pulled back in at the head of the line. The thought immediately occurred to me "Omigosh, what did I just say? That sounds to much like a challenge! How am I going to back it up?" Well it was to late now, so I just kept pushing hard on those pedals and watching my helmet mirror to see what would happen. Sure enough, after a few seconds to get over some surprise, Tom and a "crew cut' appeared to be taking up the challenge and were pulling after me. Our route soon turned into somewhat hillier terrain and I made the most of the downhill's, pulling hard on the up hills to keep from loosing speed, cutting close as I dared on the curves and checking my speedometer to see that I was holding close to a quick 33 mph on most of it. All of this was assuredly draining, but I was feeling up to it, and those guys weren't giving up! Not knowing how long I could keep up the pace, I began to wonder how I was going to get out of this impromptu race gracefully - without loosing to much face. Be assured that I was looking hard for any excuse to stop for a breath or two. Finally I saw it, one of our staff vans with a water resupply. I quickly braked to a stop near the driver and nonchalantly struck up a conversation with him. But this turned out to be a temporary staff member - a volunteer from the local biking association, who I didn't know. We didn't have much to make conversation over and nobody else was around. Tom and crew-cut came in, and we all refilled our water bottles without more than a "Hello". Then as suddenly and as smoothly as I could I jumped on the bike and peeled out. Needles to say, Tom and friend again followed. As we continued, we passed many of our friends poking along in the hot July afternoon weather. I particularly remember Don Chesterman calling from his reclining position on some body's lawn, as bikers are wan't to do in such weather. "Hey Gordon". But we did not stop. In the end we got to our camping point for the evening with me still in front. As one might expect, I had no trouble sleeping that night.

(Woody Wood #237) Woody likes to tell the story he heard just outside Bedford Pa. He says "One of our Trek cars was pulling a trailer carrying a Porta John. Our Canadian Trekker taking advantage of an opportunity began using the john. The driver returning to his vehicle and unaware that the john was being used began to pull away. Luckily he heard the Trekker screaming for him to stop and he emerged half dressed and happy to get back on his bike"

(Nancy Eislet #6) I have a comfortable feeling here at camp tonight. People are chatting, laughing, cleaning bikes, writing postcards and journals - nothing different from any other night, but I realize now that this has been "home" for 6 weeks, and in just 4 days I'll be seeing most of these folks for the last time. It's hard to believe that this odyssey is ending. In some ways it's gone so quickly, but when I reflect on all that's happened on the road it seems like an eternity.

Day 44 Bedford PA to Chambersburg PA 59 miles as remembered by Trekker's Guy Smith #280, George Gee #228 and Marianne Brems #49

(Guy Smith #280) The Bedford to Chambersburg ride was the shortest of the trip, only 58 miles. But it was billed as the toughest day of the Trek, four steep mountains, the heart of the Appalachians lay before us. I was with my favorite trio, the "Nordy" girls, Karen, Nancy and Terri. Terri still wore some bandages, but she had worked out a great system and was once again the strong, self reliant bicyclist that rode with me on the century ride back in North Dakota. We decided that the only way to conquer these mountains was to keep eating. Snack #1 came after only 16 miles on the road. We toped Blue Ridge Mountain with such ease that we were hesitant to believe the sign at the summit. Down hill we flew, only to begin climbing again. Sideling Hill wasn't to bad either, and the "Nordy" girls had fun posing for pictures in front of a sign warning about the "Dangerous Curves". We all signed a bicycle registry there, made goofy comments and had fun perusing the entries written last year by the 1988 Transamerica Trekkers. Going down a 8 percent grade was a real kick and didn't take long. Scrub Ridge was next. Luckily there was a restaurant at the summit,it was time for snack # 2. Like lightning we rode down again, and Tuscarora Mountain loomed before us. This was a four mile climb, the steepest of all, and at times the best I could do was 5 mph in my lowest granny gear. At the summit, Bridget Kneeland, one of our favorite staff members, raced the bikers on foot to the top - and usually beat them. She and her paramedic sidekick, Greg, had set up for a mountain top celebration, the end of the Appalachians. We took plenty of pictures and of course had a snack. Down the mountain we raced, cruising into Chambersburg with big smiles. It had been a great day - Fun! Jeff's memory was still with us, but all the joy of Trekking was there too. Arriving at the Chambersburg Middle school we celebrated with a snack

(George Gee #228) As we wheeled into Chambersburg Middle School grounds at 1:00 p.m., I noticed an elderly person standing at the entrance. I showered and changed and Bud Powell and I went to lunch. We returned to the school grounds and this person was still there. We went over and talked to him. He told us he read about the bicycle Trek coming to town in the local newspaper. He was there to watch us come in. He offered to give us a tour of Chambersburg. Bud and I accepted. We drove around town for around an hour and a half. He then offered to treat us to dinner. We went to a local eatery and it was the first time I ever had crab cakes Since then every time I see crab cakes on the menu, I try them. It never beats the crab cakes from Chambersburg. The name of this person is retired physician, Dr. Robert Gray. I get a card from him every year.

(Marianne Brems #49) We climbed four summits today. Checkpoint was at the top of the third. Dottie appeared there beaming in her chenille blouse. I don't think this was the most challenging day we've had even though we were told it would be. We didn't have heat and it wasn't long.

Day 45 Chambersburg PA to Lancaster PA 83 miles as remembered by Trekker Guy Smith #280 and Marianne Brems #49

NOTE: *In an article from the paper "The Bicycle Paper June 1989" Dave Shaw Trek General Manager was asked if he had any idea how much food the Trekkers might consume on the ride. Dave*

Sunrise 47

said *"the event grocery list will include:"*

- *Nearly **4 tons** of oatmeal*
- ***31,000** muffins/coffee cake*
- ***41,000** pieces of fruit*
- ***3 tons** of meat*
- ***25,000** cups of orange juice and coffee*
- ***23,000** cups of milk*
- ***38,000** pancakes*
- ***15,500** slices of bacon*
- ***18,000** eggs*
- ***10,000** potatoes*

(Guy Smith #280) Wednesday began with really crisp fresh blueberry pancakes, the best breakfast of the Trek. A large group of us rode together because we had arranged to take a tour of the Gettysburg Battlefield. It was another day to celebrate a victory over the Indiana tragedy. Jerry had convinced the mechanics to rig one of the mountain bikes with a pedestal for his broken left leg.

Pennsylvania

Jerry Wright was back on Trek, vowing to ride to Atlantic City with one leg. About 20 miles out of camp Kirk from Kansas took a bad spill on a rough railroad track, but his helmet saved his head from injury. I helped him with the first aid kit which I began carrying after my own spill in Wisconsin. I was his "angel of mercy" just as Peter had been for me. At a rest area near Gettysburg we locked up our bikes and boarded a tour bus that took us all over the historic battlefield. For two hours we heard about hero's who had given their lives or endured great suffering for a cause they believed in, both Union and Confederate. After seeing so many hero's on this bike trip, the war stories told by our guides seemed very real to me. We returned to our bikes and rode into town for lunch. I spent the rest of the day with Elle from Alaska. We decided to find another route rather than deal with the traffic and noise on busy U.S 15. Our way was longer than the trip tik route, but the quiet and serene countryside allowed us to chat and relax. At the checkpoint in East Berlin, Jerry was worn out, his right leg was cramping badly after 43 miles of hard riding. He said he would ride the sag wagon for the rest of the day, but later on I learned that he had completed the full 83 miles on the one-legged mountain bike. What a hero. Ellen was gaining a reputation as a chow hound, her fiends said that she could no longer pass food without stopping. We did stop a lot to eat. Only 4 miles away from our destination at Lancaster, my luck with tires ran out: I had my first flat since day 16 when we entered North Dakota. I still remembered how to change a tire and was soon in camp, the baseball field of McCasky High School. I spent that evening with a small group helping to organize the Trekker party for Haddon, New Jersey our last night before Atlantic City.

(Marianne Brems #49) There must have been a massive number of widows after the civil war, particularly Gettysburg. I'm curious as to why the tour guide talked so much about the blood and gore. He could have spared us and talked about the Gettysburg address.

Dawn thinks the end of Trek will be like a divorce or widowhood when it comes to the separation from people. It can't be that bad. Can it? Robin wants to know how we get ready for this. I don't think you do anymore than you get ready for a divorce or a death in the family. What I most want to bring back with me is the willingness to feel. Bruce asked me to be in his skit and play the serious introspective one. I failed in my quest to be the one who enjoys.

    We went to an Amish woman's house. The Amish woman gave us rhubarb juice and invited us in. No electricity and stark surroundings. There was running water and bottle of Vitamin C in the bathroom.

Chapter 11

Day 46 Lancaster PA to Collingswood New Jersey 74 miles as remembered by Trekker's Guy Smith #280, Mike Mitchell #1, Ellen Lowe #42 and Marianne Brems #49

(**Guy Smith #280**) It was raining again next morning as Michelle and I left Lancaster, the perfect time for another flat tire. It seemed my jinx had returned. I fixed it in the rain and then we headed into Amish country, one of the most interesting areas of our nation where old fashioned ways are preserved and honored. Here we saw small farms still worked with horse-drawn farm implements. We had plenty of room on the road because the shoulders are wide to accommodate the horse drawn carriages used by the Amish as their primary means of transportation. They also use bicycles. We got a friendly wave from everyone, especially the children, and some Trekker's were even invited into their homes. The names of the towns were as interesting as the people, along SR 340 we passed through Bird-In-Hand, Intercourse, Whitehorse and Paradise. Regretfully we left this peaceful countryside and encountered snarls of traffic along U.S. 30 one of the major thoroughfares into

Philadelphia. Heavy rains pelted us along the way, making it very difficult to see road hazards hiding under an inch of water along the roadway. Michelle and I looked liked two drowned rats when we ducked into a very nice business café to eat and warm up. Rain cools you quickly on a bicycles, we were both shivering. Fortunately it cleared a bit as we entered West Philadelphia a part of the city not known for its scenic beauty. As the hazy afternoon sun beat down, we sought an escape from the road and the traffic. We detoured to Independence square, the birthplace of United States liberty. We duly marked the occasion with pictures in front of the Liberty Bell and Independence Hall. Our next landmark was the Ben Franklin Bridge, gateway to New Jersey. There was a nice bike lane across the bridge and we had it to ourselves for a great celebration. New Jersey was our 12th and last state. We rode down Haddon Avenue past my sister Cathy's old house. And of course Cathy was there in person waiting to greet me as we turned into the Haddon Township High School. She helped me set up my tent in a soggy wet field and even went home to get me a pillow to replace mine which was water logged. Some people of Haddon volunteered to do our laundry, one of the nicest Trekker treats of the trip. I was one of the organizers of the "Trekker Talent Show" planned for that evening as our farewell party, so I set to work at once to get the stage ready. Cathy returned with some goodies and stayed to enjoy the show with us. It was an enormous success: lots of funny skits, laughter, and songs were mixed with melancholic memories of the Trek. Jeff was there in many of the offerings but in a very upbeat way. At the end we voted four people who would lead the parade into Atlantic City the next day. The votes were almost unanimous: Dottie Potts, the grandmother from Ohio, Steve Anderson, the man with multiple sclerosis, Jerry Wright riding his one-legged mountain bike, and Jim Livezey, the other Trekker from Texas who carried Jeff's number (136) on his bike as well as his own. There were many other hero's on this epic journey but these four were our choice. The party lasted two hours and ended with Nikki's "Hug Song", but it didn't have the same spontaneous effect that it did that night in Zanesville, Ohio.

(Mike Mitchell # 1) Can't remember which of the small Amish towns I stopped in today but I do remember my purpose. I have a sister (Charlene) who makes the most beautiful quilts in the world. They are truly works of art. I had heard that the Amish also made beautiful quilts so I was going to try to find one that I could have mailed back to Charlene. I went into about four shops, there were plenty of quilts to look at but they were all very plain. Charlene's were much prettier than any I looked at.So much for a good idea. I don't think I ever told Charlene about that day.

(Ellen Lowe #42) I remember Steve Anderson's struggle to accomplish his Trek goal despite his illness. The generosity of Susie Grant who had her tandem bicycle sent from New Jersey so Roger Whidden could pilot Steve to the completion of the ride.

(Marianne Brems #49) It's a place of mind giving feelings to always have one day to build on the previous days. You can't get to point C until you've gone from A and B. Real life isn't enough like that.

Trying to be organized and clean and not sweltering can be an overwhelming task. Everything is difficult. I won't miss that, but maybe some bonding with the whole experience happens at those times to. It's also difficult everyday to have to find your way around. But who cares anyway? It isn't important it's the people and the spirit that means something. The skits were wonderfully spontaneous. We did a lot with what we had at hand which was nothing.

Day 47 Collingswood NJ to Atlantic City NJ 63 miles as remembered by Trekker's Guy Smith #280, Mary Fleming #27, Jana Chapman #41, Staff Member Bridget Kneeland, Andy Rasutis #269, Roger Whidden #190, Joe Siebold #48, Hal Laster #16 and Marianne Brems #49

(Guy Smith #280) Day 47 dawned, the day nobody wanted to come, yet the one we all had waited for. Mixed feelings were everywhere as everyone wanted to ride together. I was lucky, in the course of the day I rode with many of my special friends. I started off with Team Alaska, (Ellen, Nancy and Cam) on the flat busy SR 73. We were grateful when the route switched to a much quieter two-lane rural road. Later we joined Michelle, Ellen and her daughter Shelley. I desperately wanted a large US Flag for my bike, so at the checkpoint I split from the group and rode into town to buy one for me and Michelle. We assembled at Senior Rattler's restaurant in Absecon, just 11 miles from the boardwalk. As Trekker's arrived, the air became charged with a frenzy.I remembered that Sunday afternoon in Seattle when I felt the same rumbling of excitement. Here we were 3348 miles from Seattle. We did it! Police cars led the parade. We didn't have to squeeze onto the shoulder; the whole right lane was reserved for us. We hooted and hollered, people along the way shouted to us and cars honked. It was truly a victory parade, like a triumphant Roman Army entering the city. Almost everyone wore a blue Transamerica shirt, and nothing could describe the feeling of riding in the "Long Blue Line." We stopped just short of the boardwalk so that final preparations could be made for our reception at Kennedy Center. As we waited champagne corks flew. Hugs and cheers mixed with tears. Hundreds of pictures were snapped trying to get that last shot of a inside as I chatted excitedly with special people who had become such an important part of my life in the last 47 days. In just a few moments we would be united with family and friends once again, but for one last moment we were all Trekkers a real family brought together by joys and trials. But now the moment of victory.On signal we rode up the ramp onto the boardwalk. Our own cheers were drowned out by a new crowd shouting wildly, waving banners and balloons, and cheering for us. I saw the banner first, a big sign that said. "Hey Kid Krusader" Your kids are right here". Then I saw Vicki and Shan on my own daughters, who had driven through the night from New York to be there with me. They surrounded me with hugs. Next there was Mom. with a very proud smile and a strong hug. Then came Aunt Winifred and three of their friends, my sponsors, who had taken the bus from Pennsylvania to share in this occasion. I was to busy with my family to listen to the welcome speech by the mayor of Atlantic City. But the real arrival ceremony wasn't there on the podium in Kennedy Plaza; it was in the ocean. Triumphantly I lifted my bike over my head and carried it the last few yards across the beach. Then the front wheel was lowered into the Atlantic Ocean, a symbolic gesture that completed the 3363 mile journey from the Pacific Ocean. Bicyclists cheered each other and hugged. Then began an hour-long wild party in the water. Everyone ended up in the water, Trekker's, staff, either willingly or by force. We hugged and laughed and said goodbye. Tears of joy and tears of sorrow mixed with salt water. Aching bones and sore muscles were all forgotten, but there in the ocean a new aching began. Pictures and journals are made to show others what

Transamerica Trek is all about. But for the Trekkers those 47 days are etched in our memory forever. Sometimes when I think of the bike Trek, small tears come into my eyes. I just pick up a wet towel and dry them away.

(Mary Fleming #27) Today was a very strange day. Everyone was excited to be reaching our goal but at the same time reluctant to end the experience. The ride to checkpoint was 51 miles. Jim and I rode together and I didn't feel that we were riding particularly fast but we were almost the first riders to arrive at the restaurant where checkpoint was set up.

The pain from my sore neck, acquired just before crossing the Appalachians, had migrated into my right arm, making it very difficult to keep weight on the arm. Every bump sent a shock of pain up my arm and I had to keep stopping to let it rest. In spite of all that, we made very good time, we arrived at the restaurant and just settled in for a long wait. This would be one of the last times we would all be together before we reached the crowds of family and friends at Atlantic City.

Finally at about 1 p.m. everyone had arrived including the stragglers. They got us together for pictures and we got set up for the ride into Atlantic City. We rode very slowly so that we would not lose anybody. Four bikes and riders had been chosen by the group to lead the way in. One was Jerry who had been injured in the accident and was back on the bike again. One was Dotty, an older woman rider who had impressed everyone with her "hang in there" attitude. She left camp early every day and was one of the last to come in that evening, but she never gave up. One was Roger and Steve on a tandem bike, They had started the trip separately, but Steve, who has multiple sclerosis, began to lose to much energy, so a tandem was located and they finished the ride together. The other was Jim who has been carrying Jeff's number ever since the accident to at least symbolically and in spirit get him over the finish line.

The last ten miles were ridden in formation with a police escort and a closed road. I'm amazed that there were no accidents, in such close formation for that far.

When we reached the boardwalk there was a great excitement as we waited for the staff and volunteers to get into position so that they could be a part of the final moments.

Finally, he let us on the boardwalk and we rode down to the area where they were speakers from the AlA and from the city. When we were finally released many of us headed straight for the ocean for that monumental dipping of the front wheel into the Atlantic Ocean. Ocean to ocean, coast to coast we had finally done it.

A number of riders did more than dip the wheel. I saw several bikes and riders take a total dunking. The enthusiasm level was very high. We then went to a hotel to get cleaned up and try to learn to be civilized again. We had our last mail pickup. I received several cards from supporters and a shirt with a bicyclist and "Fait Accompli 1989" on it from Mom and a lovely bouquet of flowers from the Smith's.

Later that evening we had a slide show and a party, said our goodbyes. The next day was a busy day of packing loading and catching buses to the airport.

(Jana Chapman #41) My other favorite day was meeting my boyfriend Derek on the board walk in Atlantic City. I remember Robin from Seattle laughing at me that morning after breakfast at a restaurant when she caught me trying to trim my bangs with a small pair of manicure scissors while looking in my bike mirror. I was trying to look good for Derek! Like he'd notice my bangs were long.

(Staff Member Bridgett Kneeland) Note: Bridgett rode in the 1988 Trek and is the co-writer of the song "come on, come on, do the Transamerica with me. Bridget said "I remember being in Atlantic City, on top of the van, waiting for the okay to let you guys onto the boardwalk and singing "come on, come on, do the Transamerica with me". That was the song that my sisters, Mo, Gigi and I made up for the trek. It was great helping on the trek and supporting all you guys - especially the Washingtonians! But, trekking is the best.

(Marianne Brems #49) The day started very much like any other. But the ride was flat and at mile 50, the convergence point, I arrived with energy to spare. The last 10 miles were tearful for me.

As we collected outside the Boardwalk, champagne bottles were popping everywhere and there was lot's of yelling. But as we went onto the Boardwalk things were strangely quiet. Maybe all the tourists were more interested in the fight that night. Or maybe they just didn't know who we were or care for that matter. Then came the friends and relatives of Trekkers who were very excited. Then and for the rest of the day I saw a lot of Trekkers who were very uncomfortable with the friends who came to visit them. Visitor's on trek are very awkward.

There just not Trekkers.

I think mainly everyone said goodbye in the ocean. What a wonderful feeling not to know the mileage on my car or the balance in my checking account.

(Andy Rasutis #269) One of my worst days was throwing my bike in the Atlantic Ocean when we got to the end of the ride. I fished it out, but never rode it again. It had to be done. Also having to say goodbye to my friends, I haven't cried so much in all my life. It was truly a sad moment to have to leave these people.

(Roger Whidden #190) After all the ceremonies on the boardwalk and beach, I met my wife and mom. We got pizza. I'm feeling weird - realize I have to eat outside.

That night my wife Mary and I are in our hotel room. I can't sleep in the bed - I ask if I can sleep on the floor.

Next day I'm driving the car on the Garden State Turnpike at about 20 miles per hour on the shoulder. My Mom suggests I should speed it up and get in a lane because I'm driving a car now. The trek lives on....

(Jeff Siebold #48) Arriving in Atlantic city was a mixed blessing for Trekker Jeff Siebold. He said,"A real fond event for me was my arrival on the Boardwalk in Atlantic City, New Jersey and then jumping into the Atlantic Ocean in jubilation. I also have a sad memory from that day. I lost my military ring which I had for many years and even though a lot of people helped look for it, I knew it would be a miracle if anyone were to find it, Unfortunately it is gone forever.

(Hal Laster #16) The roughest day of my life was when one of our Trekker's Jeff Green was killed by a hit-and-run driver today. The question of why did this have to happen was asked over and over, and we had our own "Trail of Tears" on this fateful day. Again the Trekker staff was wonderful. They ached as much as we did, yet they provided the leadership we needed. So forty-seven days and 3,363 miles later, I realized that the welcome sign at the hotel in Seattle had now changed in my own mind, for now I knew that the Trans America Trek was comprised of men and women, ages 17-69, who truly were "EXTRAORDINARY PEOPLE who had done AN ORDINARY THING".

Epilogue

As I was putting this book together and gathering the many accounts, I was absolutely amazed after 20 years how passionate everyone still was about this adventure. Most said this was one of the most memorable experiences of their lives. Some even went so far as to say it was life changing.

Now that you have finished reading this story, were you able to say that you got a real sense for the ride even to the point that you felt like you were a part of it?

I want to thank everyone that supported me in this effort and encouraged me to keep going. I can't believe how much I learned about the group and all of the drama and excitement that went on that I never knew about. It was impossible with 300 people to get to know everyone so this will add new information to even those who were there.

Without focusing on the tragedy of Jeff's death, I hope this book does justice to his memory.. He lives on through all of us.

As I said in the beginning, hopefully this will encourage you to take on a new challenge and push yourself a little further than you might think you can go. Thanks for reading the book (and as I always end all of my correspondence) KEEP SMILING

In Memory Of

Jeff Green

#136

Also By Michael D. Mitchell

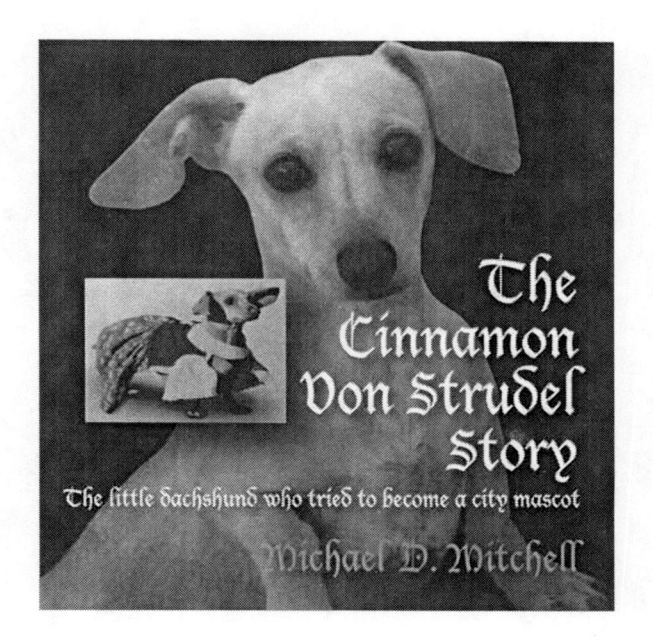

The Cinnamon Von Strudel Story
The little dachshund
who tried to become a city mascot

This is the true story about a five-year old miniature dachshund named Cinnamon Von Strudel. Follow Cinnamon's early life and brush with death, her attempt to become the first city mascot for the city of Leavenworth, Washington. Be a part of Cinnamon and her pack leader Mike's day-to-day adventures as they enjoy life and the many challenges they face.

Order at: www.cinnamonvonstrudel.com

Printed in the United States
141125LV00004B/5/P